# But *Why* Does It Work?

# But *Why* Does It Work*?*

## Mathematical Argument in the Elementary Classroom

**Susan Jo Russell**

Education Research Collaborative, TERC

**Deborah Schifter**

Education Development Center

**Reva Kasman**

Salem State University

**Virginia Bastable**

Math Leadership Programs, Mount Holyoke College

**Traci Higgins**

Education Research Collaborative, TERC

**HEINEMANN**
Portsmouth, NH

**Heinemann**
361 Hanover Street
Portsmouth, NH 03801–3912
www.heinemann.com

*Offices and agents throughout the world*

> *The authors have dedicated a great deal of time and effort to writing the content of this book, and their written expression is protected by copyright law. We respectfully ask that you do not adapt, reuse, or copy anything on third-party (whether for-profit or not-for-profit) lesson-sharing websites. As always, we're happy to answer any questions you may have.*
>
> **—Heinemann Publishers**

"Dedicated to Teachers" is a trademark of Greenwood Publishing Group, Inc.

 Preparation of this book was supported in part by the National Science Foundation under Grant No EHR-1019482. Any opinions, findings, conclusions, or recommendations expressed in this book are those of the authors and do not necessarily reflect the views of the National Science Foundation.

**Library of Congress Cataloging-in-Publication Data**
Names: Russell, Susan Jo.
Title: But why does it work? : mathematical argument in the elementary
    classroom / Susan Jo Russell [and four others].
Description: Portsmouth, NH : Heinemann, [2017]
Identifiers: LCCN 2016050433 | ISBN 9780325081144
Subjects: LCSH: Logic, Symbolic and mathematical—Study and teaching
    (Elementary). | Mathematics—Study and teaching (Elementary). | Mathematical
    analysis. | Mathematics—Philosophy.
Classification: LCC QA8.7 .B88 2017 | DDC 372.7—dc23

LC record available at https://lccn.loc.gov/2016050433

**Editor:** Katherine Bryant
**Production Editor:** Sean Moreau
**Cover Design:** Monica Ann Crigler
**Interior Design:** Shawn Girsberger
**Typesetter:** Shawn Girsberger
**Manufacturing:** Steve Bernier

Printed in the United States of America on acid-free paper
21  20  19  18  17  PPC  2  3  4  5

# CONTENTS

***But Why Does It Work?* Online Sequences**

To access the online resources for *But Why Does It Work?*, please go to www.heinemann.com and click the link in the upper right to **Log In**.

(If you do not already have an account with Heinemann, you will need to create an account.)

**Register** your product by entering the code: **WDIW**.

Once you have registered your product, it will appear in the list of **My Online Resources**.

# ACKNOWLEDGMENTS

First and foremost, we thank our collaborating teachers. Their energy, dedication, insight, and willingness to open their classrooms to us are what made the project and this book possible. The text and video examples from their classrooms in this resource are key to illustrating how students learn about mathematical argument and how teachers support that learning. We learned so much—both from observing the teachers and their students in the classroom and from the many discussions where we jointly reflected on the classroom work.

## COLLABORATING TEACHERS

| | |
|---|---|
| Tiphareth Ananda | Michele Mistalski |
| April Cannon | Lisa Nguyen |
| Stuart Clark | Anne Marie O'Reilly |
| Caitlin Doering | Lara Ramsey |
| Kathleen Drew | Karen Schweitzer |
| Nikki Faria-Mitchell | Jan Szymaszek |
| Kerri Favreau | Polly Wagner |
| Mike Flynn | Ashley Warlick |
| Matt Goldman | Sarah Weidert |
| Sarah Goodridge | Lucy Wittenberg |
| Francine Hiller | |

Joye Thaller helped us with student interviews and classroom observations, and both Joye and Amy Taber were critical in keeping on top of all the documentation.

We relied on several advisors and consultants, who reviewed our work and challenged our thinking. In particular, Jeremy Teitelbaum (University of Connecticut, Storrs) was generous with his time and perspective as a mathematician. We valued Megan Franke's (UCLA) advice throughout this work—especially her insights about student learning. And we are grateful for the advice and support from members of our advisory board and school-based advisors: Maria Blanton (TERC), Daniel Chazan (University of Maryland), Linda Davenport (Boston Public Schools), Eric Knuth (University of Wisconsin, Madison), William G. McCallum (Illustrative Mathematics), Jennifer MacPherson (Wellesley, MA, Public Schools), Christine Size (Westwood, MA, Public Schools), and Andreas J. Stylianides (University of Cambridge).

# INTRODUCTION

I n a second-grade class, students are sharing solutions to the following problem:

> *Craig and Luisa were playing a game with 52 pennies. Craig hid some of the pennies, and then there were 29 showing. How many did Craig hide?*

The teacher asks Henry and Melissa to share their solutions first, because she knows they have quite different strategies. Henry subtracted 29 from 52, and Melissa added up from 29 to 52. The teacher wonders if students will understand why both strategies work. She thinks this discussion might also be an opportunity to engage students in thinking explicitly about the relationship between addition and subtraction.

**Henry:** I wanted to figure out how many pennies are left if you take away 29. So I subtracted 20 from 52, so that's 32. Then I had to subtract 9 more, but it was easier to subtract 10 and then add 1 back, so I got 22, then $22 + 1 = 23$.

**Melissa:** I did it a different way. I said $29 + 1$ is 30. Then you need 22 more to get to 52.

**Teacher: Does anyone have questions about Henry's or Melissa's solutions?**

**Alberto:** I don't agree with Melissa. She said she got 22, but I got 23 like Henry.

**Teacher: Melissa, do you understand Alberto's thinking? Do you want to explain your solution?**

**Melissa:** The answer isn't 22. That was only how I got from 30 to 52. My answer is 23.

**Henry:** I don't understand how you got your answer either. You were adding, and I think we should be subtracting.

**Teacher: Melissa, explain a little more about how you figured out that 23 pennies were hidden. I noticed you had a picture with your work. It might help to use your picture to explain your thinking.**

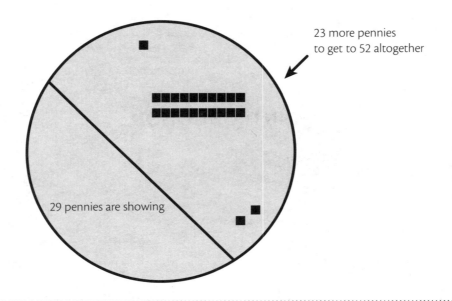

23 more pennies
to get to 52 altogether

29 pennies are showing

**All 52 Pennies**

**Melissa [showing her picture]:** This whole circle is all 52 pennies. I didn't draw all the pennies; it's just like a pile of 52. So 29 of them are showing. That means I have to see how many pennies it takes to get up to 52, so first I added on 1—that's this little square—now we're up to 30. Then you add on 20, then you're up to 50, that's these two tens right here. Then you add on 2 more. So you had to add on 1, then 20, then 2, that's 23 altogether that are hidden.

**Henry and some other students:** Oooh!

**Henry:** I get it. I started at 52 and took away the 29 part. Melissa started with the 29 and added up to figure out the part to get up to 52. It comes out the same.

**Teacher: So how come Henry can solve this problem with subtraction and Melissa can solve it with addition? I'd like you to think more about this, and we're going to come back to this question in our next session.**

The teacher recognizes that, through their discussion, her students are beginning to make explicit an important mathematical idea that some of them already use implicitly in their work: Any problem that can be solved by subtraction can also be solved by finding a missing addend and vice versa. In her next lesson, she plans to present more examples of this relationship and to ask students to talk about what they notice about this relationship across multiple examples.

Through this opening discussion, students are working on both mathematical content and mathematical practices. As they present their solution strategies, they are not only showing how they got an answer to the problem, but, with the guidance of their teacher, they are learning to engage in the practice of constructing mathematical arguments. In the elementary grades, representations are central to argumentation in mathematics. The teacher asks Melissa to use her picture while articulating her argument to help other students understand her reasoning.

Mathematical argument—the focus of this book—is not just for solving individual problems. By the end of this discussion, the teacher is asking students to begin considering something more *general* about the behavior of the operations, something that applies to a whole class of problems, in this case, the relationship between addition and subtraction. As the class continues to discuss this idea, they will learn to articulate a conjecture about the relationship between subtracting and finding a missing addend and will use representations as the basis for their mathematical arguments about why it occurs.

> *"Mathematically, the math argument routines position the operations as central. Students have developed comfort and curiosity about what the operations mean and how these can be examined closely. It has now become routine for students on their own to bring up questions or observations about the operations."*
>
> [GRADE 3 TEACHER}

Until recently, mathematical argument did not have a central presence in the elementary mathematics curriculum. In fact, in our work over the past decade at the intersection of research and practice, we found that most elementary teachers did not have experience with mathematical argument themselves and had even less experience incorporating mathematical argument into their classrooms. At the same time, documents such as *Adding It Up* (National Research Council 2001), *Principles to Actions* (National Council of Teachers of Mathematics 2014), and the *Common Core State Standards: Mathematics* (National Governors Association Center for Best Practices 2010) have been emphasizing the importance of mathematical justification and argument as a core mathematics practice, resulting in a greater push by schools, school systems, and new assessments to make it a focus in the math classroom.

We chose to focus our work on mathematical argument in the content area of number and operations, in part because number and operations constitute core content in the elementary grades but also because we noticed how often, within their work on calculation, students came up with ideas that led to opportunities to develop mathematical arguments about the behavior of the operations. For example, in the previous dialogue, the students notice that a problem that can be solved by subtraction can also be solved as a missing addend problem. As another example, young students learning their addition facts use strategies that can be generalized: "I know $6 + 6 = 12$, so $6 + 7$ has to be 13." The student is not yet making an argument but is noticing a relationship, one that can be extended beyond the specific numbers and expressed as a generalization that "has to" be true. We have come to recognize this kind of statement as different from simply asserting a correct mathematical fact such as "$6 + 7$ equals 13." The statement implies a general idea about the operation of addition—that if you add 1 to an addend, the sum also increases by 1. While a great deal of reasoning and representing is required to move from that initial statement about the relationship of $6 + 7$ to $6 + 6$ to a general

> *"Students have found ways to pull the mathematical argument work into our everyday work. They say things like, 'Will we be making a conjecture about this?' and 'I have proof to explain why this works.' Students also used the ideas that we covered in the math argument lessons to help them complete the math in our regular program. 'This is just like our conjecture,' was something I heard about our study of multiplication."*
>
> [GRADE 4 TEACHER]

claim about addition, this kind of observation is an excellent starting point for work on mathematical argument.

We wrote this book to provide teachers with practical support for a focus on mathematical argument about the operations in elementary classrooms. It is the product of the authors' collaboration with twenty-one teachers over three school years to develop a teaching model for engaging students in mathematical argument. During this time, the teachers met periodically to examine and engage in mathematical argument themselves and to share their observations about mathematical argument in their classrooms. Together, staff and teachers studied videotapes of classroom sessions as well as the teachers' own written accounts of their students' investigations.

As a result of this work, we developed a teaching model that consists of five phases: (1) noticing a pattern or regularity; (2) articulating a claim about that regularity; (3) investigating what has been noticed and articulated through the use of representations; (4) constructing a mathematical argument about why the regularity occurs; and (5) comparing what occurs in one operation with what occurs in similar circumstances with another operation. These phases will be described more fully in Chapters 3 and 4. We also developed eight different lesson sequences, based on the teaching model, which the collaborating teachers implemented and refined in their classrooms.

The next sections describe what you will find in this book and accompanying resources.

## CONTENT OF THE BOOK

Chapter 1, "Mathematical Argument in the Elementary Grades: What and Why?," introduces the major content of the book—the focus on mathematical argument, why that's important, and the choice of operations as a context for work on mathematical argument for elementary students. The chapter introduces the concept of "productive lingering" on important mathematics. Chapter 2, "Elementary Students as Mathematicians," describes how students engage in "new to them" mathematics and how their work parallels the process by which professional mathematicians create mathematical ideas. Chapter 3, "The Teaching Model," presents the teaching model for engaging students in mathematical argument, describes the five phases in detail, and presents classroom examples to illustrate how each phase engages students in important mathematical ideas and practices. Chapter 4, "Using the Lesson Sequences: What the Teacher Does," details where the teacher focuses her attention, the decisions she makes in response to students' thinking, and the actions she takes as the class goes through the fives phases of the teaching model. Chapter 5, "Mathematical Argument in the Elementary Classroom: Impact on Students and Teachers," summarizes evidence from student assessments and classroom observations about what students in our collaborating classrooms learned about mathematics content and practices, what was gained in participation and confidence, and how students applied their learning about mathematical argument in their regular math classes.

Chapters 1 through 4 also include video- and text-based examples drawn from the classrooms of our collaborating teachers; mathematical investigations for you to develop your own mathematical thinking and to become familiar with the mathematics content students in the examples are working on; and sets of focus questions about selected examples and about each chapter as a whole.

This book can be read by individuals or used as the basis of a study group for teachers and teacher educators. Whether you are reading this book by yourself or with a group, we encourage you to do the mathematical investigations, even if the ideas seem familiar to you at first. By considering your own responses, you will be better prepared to understand the range of student responses in the examples. In some instances, the suggested problems will ask you to go more deeply into the mathematics than what the elementary students are doing so that you investigate a broader mathematical context and develop a sense of where the students' explorations might go. The focus questions are designed to give you time to pause and reflect on both the students' thinking and the teachers' moves.

## CLASSROOM EXAMPLES: TEXT AND VIDEO

Examples from our classrooms illustrate Chapters 1 through 4. Our schools included public schools in urban centers, as well as suburban and rural towns, and a university-based private school. Some of the classrooms have significant numbers of special needs students, ESL students, and/or students from low-income families. They include students with a history of excelling in math and on state assessments and students who have had difficulty with grade-level mathematics and performed poorly on state assessments.

> *"The Algebra and Proof sessions have established a framework for discussing mathematics and a set of expectations for working collaboratively to examine mathematical problems and situations."*
>
> [GRADE 2 TEACHER]

We gathered these examples in two ways. First, teachers regularly wrote episodes about classroom lessons, including: a description of the activity; an account of students' words, actions, and representations; and reflections by the teacher about students' learning and her own teaching. We also videotaped selected lessons in each classroom. Examples detailed in the book are drawn from both written and video examples; some are composites of events in several classrooms.

To get the most out of each chapter, we suggest that you stop and watch each video clip when it comes up in the chapter. Readers often find it useful to view a video once through to get a sense of the whole episode. Then view it a second time, stopping at the indicated pauses to consider the focus questions for each section. For all the examples, whether text or video, we urge you to pay close attention to each student's thinking, the collective thinking of the class, and how each teacher elicits and supports students' ideas.

To access the video components, please refer to the in-text URLs and QR codes.

## THE LESSON SEQUENCES ON MATHEMATICAL ARGUMENT

The authors and collaborating teachers developed and field-tested the eight lesson sequences on mathematical argument over two complete school years in a variety of classrooms. Each sequence is intended to be implemented as a series of short sessions over the course of a semester in the way that many teachers use classroom routines or number talks in addition to their regular math classes. Each lesson sequence is a coherent series of about twenty to twenty-five sessions, with each session taking about 15 to 20 minutes. Field-test teachers implemented one sequence each semester by doing these sessions two or three times per week, finding time at the beginning of the day, as part of morning meeting, just before or after lunchtime, or at the end of the school day. As the year went on, some teachers discovered that the work was closely connected to their core curriculum and used the activities right before or after their math lessons.

> "Over the course of the year I have found that my approach to certain units or lessons has changed as a result of my work with the Algebra and Proof sequences. I am much more likely to support students to answer their own questions by encouraging the use of manipulatives, story problems, and representations. I am finding that I am asking better questions, which will ultimately guide my students to richer and deeper understanding."
>
> [GRADE 2 TEACHER]

Teachers found it was important to give these lesson sequences a special name so that students knew when they were turning to this work. They might be called Constructing Mathematical Argument lessons or Making and Proving Conjectures. Because of the focus on how the operations behave, some of our collaborating teachers called them Algebra and Proof lessons. The properties and behaviors of the operations fall into the content area of early algebra: they work in the same way whether the elements are numbers or algebraic symbols, thus linking arithmetic and algebra. Whatever name you choose for these lessons, referring to them consistently helps the class track these lessons as a coherent progression.

In each lesson sequence on mathematical argument, students work with two or three related general claims. The table in the appendix provides the content of each sequence, how you can access it, at which grade levels it might be used, and, if it is illustrated in the book, which chapters contain examples from that sequence. Two of these sequences, Same Sum, Same Difference (Whole Numbers) and Changing a Number in Addition or Multiplication (Whole Numbers), can be found in the appendix. These two sequences are referred to frequently in Chapters 3 and 4, respectively.

Please refer to page vi for directions to access all eight online sequences.

You can use the sequences that involve addition and subtraction in any grade, while those that involve multiplication and division should be used after students have developed some familiarity

**Connecting Arithmetic to Algebra**
This book is a companion volume to *Connecting Arithmetic to Algebra: Strategies for Building Algebraic Thinking in the Elementary Grades* (*CAA*). That volume laid out the territory of engaging young students in mathematical argument, illustrated with rich examples from teachers' own classroom accounts. If you have read *CAA*, then this volume provides more substantial guidance and specific curricular material for incorporating this work into your instruction throughout the school year. If you're starting with this volume, you may want to read *CAA* later or use it as a reference for more of a foundation in the mathematics and further examples of classroom episodes. *CAA* also includes chapters on issues such as: how the range of learners in the classroom participate in this work; using symbolic notation; and looking ahead to middle school.

with those operations. Because students are dealing with the new and complex practice of constructing arguments, the size of the numbers should be familiar and accessible throughout most of the sequence. Students need to be able to generate and manipulate examples and representations without becoming bogged down in computation that is too difficult for them.

These sequences provide a focused, structured, coherent approach to implementing work on mathematical argument about the operations into the elementary classroom. They use general claims that we have found to be accessible and productive for students. The lesson sequences are intended to be a flexible framework that teachers can shape in response to their own students' ideas and the pace of their work. For example, teachers often stretched a single lesson over several sessions. The lessons are not a curriculum but a structure that guides you and your students through the five phases of the teaching model. Once you are familiar with this approach, the five phases provide a template for study of other general claims that are brought up by students or that you choose because they are relevant to the mathematical content your class is studying. Teachers found that the dedicated time spent working through a mathematical argument lesson sequence resulted in students developing the habits of noticing patterns and regularities, making conjectures about what they noticed, and using representations to construct arguments, and that these habits positively impacted students' work in their regular mathematics curriculum.

# 1

# Mathematical Argument in the Elementary Grades: What and Why?

As elementary students work on core mathematics content about number and operations, some begin to use key properties and behaviors of the operations implicitly as they solve problems. For example, third graders who are encouraged to think about using what they know to solve problems might solve $4 \times 9$ by reasoning from a more familiar fact, as happens in this classroom dialogue.

**Johann:** I know $4 \times 10$ is 40, so $4 \times 9$ has to be 4 less, that's 36.

**Teacher: What do you think about Johann's reasoning? Do you agree?**

**Evie:** I think it has to work because, if you think of it like you have four groups of 10, then you'd have to take 1 away from each group. Then it's four 9s.

**Teacher: I see some people agreeing and some people not sure. Can anyone say more about what Johann and Evie are saying?**

**Ada:** Can I show something? See, here are four sticks of 10. That's 40, right? Here's how I make it $4 \times 9$. Just take 1 cube off each stack. That's 40 subtract 4, so it has to be 36.

**Natalie:** Oooh, I get it. You take 1 away every time you make a 10 into a 9. And it would work with anything times 10 and times 9. It would be the same for 20 times 10 and 20 times 9, except you'd have to take away 20 instead of 4 because you'd have 20 stacks.

We often hear students engage in reasoning about numbers and operations, but when their reasoning is correct, as Johann's is, it may be accepted without any further questioning. If the idea underlying the student's reasoning is not made explicit, the opportunity for all students to engage in such thinking is lost. The journey from thinking through one example, such as using $4 \times 10$ as a starting point for solving $4 \times 9$, to clearly stating and justifying a general claim about a whole class of examples that behave in the same way is what this book is about. This journey focuses on constructing mathematical arguments about the behavior of the operations.

## THE WHAT: REPRESENTATION-BASED ARGUMENT

The examples in this book focus on *representation-based arguments*. Representations—physical models, drawings, diagrams such as number lines or arrays, and story contexts—are the primary tools available to elementary students as they construct mathematical arguments. In the previous example, Ada presents a representation to support Johann's reasoning. She shows 4 sticks, each consisting of 10 connecting cubes to represent $4 \times 10$, then removes 1 cube from each stick, a total of 4 cubes, to change $4 \times 10$ to $4 \times 9$.

$$4 \times 10 = 40$$

$$4 \times 9 = (4 \times 10) - 4 = 36$$

Ada's argument is about a specific example. Natalie is thinking about how to generalize Ada's representation to represent a larger class of problems—she seems to be saying that any number of stacks of 10 represents "anything times 10" and that taking 1 cube off each stack results in that same number of stacks times 9.

A representation-based argument includes not only the picture, story context, or physical model but also the words and actions the student uses. For example, Ada's words, "Just take 1 cube off each stack," and her gestures in removing those cubes, are important components of her argument. The combination of the representation and the words and actions that describe it creates a dynamic explanation.

We might infer from Ada's contribution to the previous dialogue that students in this classroom take for granted that representations are a central part of argumentation in mathematics. From Natalie's remarks, we might infer that students are used to generalizing from particular examples to what is true for a larger class of problems. But even if all of this is true, it's unlikely that all students are following Ada's and Natalie's thinking. Students don't learn to construct or to understand such representation-based arguments without a focused, coherent series of activities that immerses students in the mathematical ideas. They need time to consider these arguments and to think through how the representation works with multiple examples. In this chapter, we consider how teachers begin to develop a focus on mathematical argument in their classrooms.

### Mathematical Argument and Productive Lingering

At a meeting toward the end of our project, the collaborating teachers were trying to describe what characterized their sessions about mathematical argument and why these lessons had been so productive for the students in their classes. One of the teachers talked about the importance of "lingering" on important ideas in these sessions in a way that encouraged students to think deeply about the mathematics. Other teachers resonated with the word *lingering*. They talked about how, in their regular math classes, they often felt pressured to move ahead quickly, to keep up with their school's curriculum or pacing guide. In contrast, their Math Argument or Algebra and Proof sessions had a different pace. "Lingering" on students' ideas about important mathematics content had, they asserted, enabled their students to engage with mathematical ideas fundamental to their study of numbers and operations.

We have continued to think about what we call "productive lingering" in the following three areas. Each area is characterized by central questions that students consider while engaging in mathematical argument.

- Lingering on examples: What do you notice? Is there an underlying pattern or regularity?

- Lingering on articulating the regularity: Can you describe what you notice? Can you articulate a conjecture? What's the "it" that we're making an argument about?

- Lingering on investigating structure through representation: How can you use a representation to show what is happening? How are the elements of the conjecture, including the action of the operation, shown in the representation? How does it show what changes and what stays the same? Can you use the representation to show specific examples? Can you use it to construct a general argument?

## EXAMPLES OF MATHEMATICAL ARGUMENT

In this chapter, we provide glimpses of what it looks like when elementary students and their teachers engage in learning to construct mathematical arguments about the operations. We use three video examples to highlight important aspects of this work. As you consider the examples, think about how students are engaged in the three aspects of productive lingering.

These examples will also introduce you to sessions from two of the online lesson sequences: Core Ideas of Addition and Subtraction and Changing a Number in Addition or Subtraction. The examples do not illustrate every aspect of mathematical argument or every phase of the teaching model that we will be discussing in Chapters 3 and 4; they are intended to give you glimpses, and we will provide more detail in those chapters.

Each example contains a mathematical investigation for you to do to acquaint yourself with the mathematics content and the kind of thinking students are doing. As you watch and read about the examples, notice how the students are considering the operation as an object of study, how they build on particular examples in order to move toward saying something general about the operation, and how the teachers support students to consider how an operation behaves across multiple problems.

### Example 1: Noticing a Pattern in Addition

#### MATHEMATICAL INVESTIGATION

Examine these pairs of related addition equations:

| | |
|---|---|
| $12 + 8 = 20$  <br>$14 + 8 = 22$ | $12 + 8 = 20$  <br>$12 + 10 = 22$ |
| $38 + 45 = 83$  <br>$43 + 45 = 88$ | $38 + 45 = 83$  <br>$38 + 50 = 88$ |

What generalization about addition is suggested by the change from the first equation to the second equation in each pair?
What generalization fits the first row of problems?
What generalization fits all of the problems?

Write out your generalization using everyday language; some people find using terms like *addend* and *sum* useful. Using counters, a drawing, a number line, or a story context, explain why this generalization must be true, no matter what addition expression you start with. How does addition show up in your representation? How do the changes from the first equation to the second show up in your representation?

In this example, a fourth-grade teacher uses a set of addition problems to lay the groundwork for engaging her students in mathematical argument. At the beginning of the video, the teacher and her class review what a student's responsibility is when the student doesn't understand what another student says. We'll focus on the next part of the video that starts as the students first consider the following pairs of problems:

| | |
|---|---|
| $12 + 8 = 20$  <br>$14 + 8 = 22$ | $12 + 8 = 20$  <br>$12 + 10 = 22$ |
| $38 + 45 = 83$  <br>$43 + 45 = 88$ | $38 + 45 = 83$  <br>$38 + 50 = 88$ |

The teacher asks the students what they notice and suggests they might make a conjecture about what is going on in pairs of problems like these.

---

## FOCUS QUESTIONS

**VIDEO 1.1, SECTION 1**  Why does the teacher ask students to rearticulate the ideas expressed by other students? What is added by each explanation?

Why do you think the teacher checks back with Liam about the way she has recorded his idea?

**VIDEO 1.1, SECTION 2**  Why do you think the teacher asks other students to restate Liam's rule? What do you notice about students' responses to this question?

**VIDEO 1.1, SECTION 3**  How does Naomi's conjecture differ from Liam's (which is recorded when it's restated by Brage)?

Students offer different questions about Naomi's conjecture. Why might the teacher choose to focus on "Can you give an example?"

What might be the teacher's intention in asking students to write at the end of the lesson?

Video
1.1 ▶

http://hein.pub/WDIW1.1

As we mentioned in the Introduction, it is often useful to view a video once all the way through in order to familiarize yourself with the episode, then view it a second time, stopping to consider the focus questions at the end of each section.

...................................................................

The fourth graders begin by noticing how the equations in each pair are related and trying to describe what they are noticing. As you can see from different students' attempts to put their ideas into words, describing a mathematical pattern clearly is in itself a challenging enterprise. Students build on and revise each other's ideas until they have two statements that the teacher records: "If you add 2 to one addend, the sum has to be 2 more," and then the expanded conjecture, "If you add any number to an addend, then your sum will be as much as you added more." Throughout the class, the teacher asks students to talk through their conjectures using examples, and we hear other students' "Ohs" of comprehension or "Now I get it" when examples are explicated. As the class ends, the teacher asks students to briefly record their thoughts individually, so that they have one more chance to capture where their ideas are after this discussion and so that she can see the range of thinking in her class. The class will continue to refine their conjecture and will then work on constructing arguments using representations to model their ideas.

### Example 2: Articulating a Rule About Subtraction

**MATHEMATICAL INVESTIGATION**

Examine these pairs of related subtraction equations:

| | |
|---|---|
| $8 - 3 = 5$<br>$9 - 3 = 6$ | $8 - 3 = 5$<br>$8 - 4 = 4$ |
| $10 - 4 = 6$<br>$11 - 4 = 7$ | $10 - 4 = 6$<br>$10 - 5 = 5$ |

What generalizations about subtraction are suggested by this set of equations?

Write out your generalizations. Using counters, a drawing, a number line, or a story context, explain why these generalizations must be true, no matter what subtraction expression you start with.

In this third-grade classroom, students have previously studied what happens to the sum when an addend is increased, beginning like the students in the previous clip and then going on to develop conjectures and construct arguments about that behavior of addition. Now they have been working on what happens to the difference when they change the first number in a subtraction expression. The third graders already have a clear understanding of how changing an addend affects the sum. But when students make generalizations about an operation, especially when they are dealing with the familiar operation of addition, they may assume their generalization works for any operation.

After the students try examples and work in small groups to describe what they have observed, the teacher brings them together to share their ideas. In this phase of their investigation, she asks them to articulate a rule about subtraction, based on their work so far. Even though students have ideas about what is going on, it takes time to articulate these ideas clearly, requiring trying out language and then revising it. As you watch the video, think about how making the effort to put their ideas into words supports students in gaining clarity about what they've noticed.

## ▌FOCUS QUESTIONS

Video 1.2 ▶

http://hein.pub/WDIW1.2

**VIDEO 1.2, SECTION 1**  The teacher writes down what the students offer verbatim, without correcting them or asking for clarification. Why might she choose to do that?

**VIDEO 1.2, SECTION 2**  Why might the teacher choose to pause to have the class consider Manea's example of 50 − 10 and 40 − 10? What do the students' responses contribute to the discussion?

In this video, the teacher encourages the class to focus on putting the generalization they notice into words to come to a common understanding of the idea. The teacher allows students to take the time they need to articulate their ideas in their own ways. By eliciting and recording different ways to express their rule, she gives students the chance to listen to different formulations and compare them to their own. This provides an opportunity for students to capture their ideas in a clear, precise, and unambiguous way. They are learning how to communicate about *general* mathematical ideas. When Manea offers an example, the teacher encourages students to use the example to clarify their articulations. By the end of the class, Sarah and Tyshaun are beginning to make arguments about why their generalization is true. After the students have formulated a clear statement of their conjecture, they will work on developing their arguments more fully, using representations. Eventually they will compare their findings about changing the first number in a subtraction expression to changing the second number in a subtraction expression.

### Example 3: Using the Structure of a Representation to Construct an Argument

#### MATHEMATICAL INVESTIGATION

| | |
|---|---|
| $3 + 4 = 7$ | $48 + 37 = 85$ |
| $4 + 3 = 7$ | $37 + 48 = 85$ |

What generalization about addition do these pairs of equations illustrate?

Write it down as clearly as you can. You might recognize that these are examples of the commutative property of addition, but it is not sufficient to write, "This is the commutative property of addition"; you should describe what is changing, what is staying the same, and how those are related.

In a second-grade class, students have been discussing how the order of two addends can be reversed, but the sum stays the same. As class begins on this day, the teacher draws their attention to the poster from the previous session on which they recorded their ideas.

Our conjecture:

It has to be adding.

It has to be the two same numbers but opposite.

When you add, you can switch them around and have the same answer.

If you have 9 and 3 all you have to do is switch them around and they equal the same number.

In these beginning articulations, students have captured key points about the commutative property of addition. The first statement indicates that the operation they are considering is addition—while this may seem obvious at first, we have found that students don't necessarily see a conjecture as specific to an operation (this issue will be discussed further in Chapters 3 and 4). The second statement specifies that the numbers in the two different addition expressions have to be the same numbers. Both this statement and the next statement, using different words, talk about changing the order of the numbers. Although the word *opposite* is ambiguous, the third sentence clarifies what it means. The third statement connects the premise to the conclusion—that the result of changing the order of the numbers is that the sum doesn't change. The fourth clarifies the referents by providing an example with specific numbers. Each statement contributes something to the students' collective understanding of what operation they are considering, what is changing, what remains the same, and how the value of the sum is related to the change of order of the addends. The four statements together create a complete conjecture.

Once they have reviewed their ideas, the teacher asks what would happen if they were adding three numbers, for example $2 + 3 + 4$. If the order of the addends is changed, will the sum still be the same? The students investigate this idea in pairs for a few minutes. The teacher encourages them to use representations as part of their investigation, and then brings them back together to share their explanations and representations.

In the first section of the clip, you will see the teacher introducing the session. The next section shows the students' discussion after they have worked in pairs on their ideas about changing the order of three addends. This section begins just after a student has said, "If there was $2 + 3 + 4$, it would be the same, and then if you switch them around they will be the same numbers. It would be the same amount of kids because you're not taking any away or putting anymore there." The teacher asks if other students can say this in their own words. The clip opens as Lilliana responds.

Video 1.3 ▶

http://hein.pub/WDIW1.3

## ❙ FOCUS QUESTIONS

**VIDEO 1.3, SECTION 1**   How does the teacher help the students connect the day's activity to their previous work?

**VIDEO 1.3, SECTION 2**   How does Olivia represent addition? How does she show that the sum doesn't change if the order of the addends is changed? How does her language indicate that she is talking about addition in general, not just $2 + 3 + 4$?

Liliana gives a clear explanation at the beginning of this clip. Olivia also provides a clear explanation, using her representation. Why does the teacher continue to ask for other students' ways of thinking about the same idea after each of their contributions?

**VIDEO 1.3, SECTION 3**   Why do you think the teacher introduces larger numbers? How do different students respond to her questions about whether the idea works with larger numbers?

**AT THE END OF THE VIDEO:**   What does the teacher do to support students to interact with each other's ideas throughout the lesson?

How does the teacher create a discussion that includes students with a range of strengths and experience in the same conversation? How are different students working on differ-ent aspects of the content?

················································································

Some students express their idea that the order of the addends doesn't change the sum. Liliana makes an argument, relying on a description of the actions involved. Then Olivia shows her argument, using a representation of stacks of cubes held on her fingers. She demonstrates what Liliana said by turning her hand around to change the order of the stacks. While she acknowledges that the sum is 9 when she changes the order, she talks primarily in general terms, as if her stacks of cubes could represent any amount: "I would know it's the same number 'cause you just turn them around."

As the conversation continues, some students think about the *general* idea of changing the order of the addends, while others suggest different orders for the specific quantities, 2, 3, and 4. When the teacher offers an example with numbers that students can't easily add in their heads, $86 + 92 + 105$, some students are convinced that these numbers, too, can be reordered without affecting the sum. But other students go back to the smaller numbers, continuing to linger on examples as they develop images of what is happening to the addends and the sum. It is a conversation that allows for a range of students to participate and to investigate the behavior of addition, both with particular examples and in more general terms.

### Characteristics of Representation-Based Arguments

In the last video, Olivia's explanation is a representation-based argument. The following three characteristics are key to successful representation-based arguments:

1. *The action and meaning of the operation is clearly represented.* Olivia shows the three addends as separate stacks and talks about and demonstrates joining them together. For example, when she wraps her hand around all three stacks, she shows the meaning of addition as joining quantities.

2. *The representation is not just about specific quantities but can be used to show what happens with "any numbers" or some set of numbers that students are working with.* Depending on students' experience, this set might be whole numbers up to some value, or all whole numbers, or whole numbers and fractions, and so forth. Although Olivia holds a specific number of cubes, stacks of 2, 3, and 4, she talks about the stacks in general terms: "I would know it's *the same number* cause you just turn them around."

3. *The representation shows why the conjecture must be true; the structure of the representation shows how the conclusion of the claim follows from its premise.* In this example, the premise is that the order of addends is changed; the conclusion is that the sum doesn't change. Olivia's representation shows, simultaneously, changing the order of addends and keeping the sum the same.

Olivia's representation-based argument consists of the stacks of cubes along with the words and actions she uses to describe the representation. For example, the way Olivia turns the cubes around and her explanation that "you never gave any away, you never added more" are integral parts of her argument. Using her words and actions, she connects the cube representation to the class conjecture.

In the elementary grades, students often do not construct a complete representation-based argument on their own. The work on articulating and proving conjectures is collaborative, with students comparing representations and building on each other's ideas. All students can *participate* in a discussion about proving, each student bringing her or his own resources and engaging at the edge of her or his understanding. While some students are thinking through how a representation can be viewed to make an argument for all whole numbers, other students may be thinking about specific cases and deepening their understanding of the structure of the operation that is the focus of the generalization.

Representations in the form of physical models, drawings, diagrams, number lines, arrays, and story contexts are students' tools for thinking and communicating. Representations allow students to make connections among the elements of their conjecture, the numbers and symbols in the expressions or equations that are examples of that conjecture, and the relationships defined by the operation. The representations help students recognize and justify *why* the symbol patterns they have noticed work. You will encounter more examples of students' representation-based arguments in Chapters 2 through 4.

## WHY LINGER ON MATHEMATICAL ARGUMENT?

The three examples provide glimpses of the kind of work students can do when they are given opportunities to notice, articulate, represent, and justify generalizations about the operations. Why is it worth spending precious classroom time on mathematical argument about the operations?

### *Focus on the Operations*

First, the mathematics content of these lessons focuses on the properties and behaviors of the operations. An operation is not only a set of directions to compute. It is also a mathematical object that has its own properties and behaviors. These properties and behaviors underlie all written computation and mental arithmetic strategies and are crucial to understanding arithmetic and, later, algebra.

Much has been learned over the past few decades about focusing on making sense in all aspects of mathematics content. In many classrooms, students are expected to understand and justify their computation strategies rather than simply follow a series of memorized steps. But even with this increased focus on meaning, the teaching of number and operations is often largely restricted to learning calculation strategies to solve specific problems. As a result, many students view the operations as only instructions to do computation rather than mathematical objects that embody certain actions and have their own properties and behaviors. Students do not have the opportunity or guidance to focus on the operations as objects of study.

Understanding how an operation behaves is critical mathematics content. In the context of computation, when students have not had the opportunity to think deeply about the properties and behaviors of addition, subtraction, multiplication, and division, they are less likely to be able to assess the expected magnitude of their results before embarking on calculation or to recognize the reasonableness or unreasonableness of their solutions. When students later encounter these same operations in algebra, they haven't developed a strong foundation to draw on to make meaning for expressions and equations with variables.

For example, the mathematical idea that Olivia and her classmates are working on in Example 3 on the previous page—that changing the order of addends does not change the sum— may seem very simple, yet it has profound implications for work in both arithmetic and algebra. These students are working with ideas related to what mathematicians refer to as the commutative and associative properties of addition. They begin by thinking with small whole numbers and then consider whether their ideas hold true for larger whole numbers. Through the grades, they will learn how this and other properties apply to whole numbers, fractions, integers, and, later, to algebraic expressions. And by developing arguments about these properties of addition (and in a later grade, multiplication), they can better see why they *cannot* reverse terms in a subtraction expression or the dividend and divisor in a division expression.

Elementary students don't need to know the names or formal definitions of these properties to make sense of ideas like those they are working with in the videos. But through studying examples and using representations, students are learning to articulate the ideas for themselves, to understand why they make sense, and to recognize when and how they apply. While some students notice and use these behaviors on their own, they may not understand their significance or their generality. Other students never notice them or notice them in some situations but fail to recognize other situations where they apply. Making study of these behaviors explicit gives students the opportunity to expand their understanding of the meaning and structure of the operations and to apply this understanding when they encounter new types of numbers or mathematical symbols.

### Mathematical Practices

Second, a focus on mathematical argument opens a gateway for young students into learning about central mathematical practices. Our classroom examples show how students engage in these practices, including: noticing patterns and regularities; articulating what they notice and making conjectures; using pictures, diagrams, physical models, and story contexts to represent the structure of mathematical relationships; and constructing arguments using those representations. These practices are also highlighted in the mathematical practices of the Common Core State Standards. When students look for patterns across multiple problems, they are engaged in Math Practice 8, *Look for and express regularity in repeated reasoning*. This is the first phase of the teaching model presented in this book (see page xii in the Introduction). When they articulate a conjecture or clarify their ideas in discussion, they are enacting Math Practice 6, *Attend to precision*. While this practice occurs during all phases of their work on mathematical argument, it is particularly present in the second phase. The creation and use of representations in constructing arguments about the operations is a demonstration of Math Practice 7, *Look for and make use of structure*. This practice is especially a focus in phases 3, 4, and 5 of the teaching model. And, of course, the entire focus of this work is on Math Practice 3, *Construct viable arguments and critique the reasoning of others*. (For more on the Mathematical Practices, see the elementary elaborations of the CCSS Math Practices at www.illustrativemathematics.org/standards/practice. Also see Michael Flynn's *Beyond Answers: Exploring Mathematical Practices with Young Children*.)

### Authentic Mathematical Work

Third, when students have the opportunity to notice regularities and develop their own conjectures and arguments about them, they seem to recognize that what they are doing is challenging and authentic mathematical work. Because the actual computation often involves familiar, manageable numbers, students with a wide range of experience and prior success in mathematics can work together on these foundational ideas about how operations behave. The video examples in this chapter include students who are diverse in terms of academic achievement, socioeconomic status, and language and cultural background. According to their teachers, students who contributed substantively to the math ideas in these discussions included students who generally excel in grade-level computation and those struggling with grade-level computation; students at ease with reading and writing as well as English language learners; and students who are confident in their mathematical performance and those who started the school year unsure of themselves.

### *The Importance of Lingering*

The three video episodes in this chapter illustrate "productive lingering" on examples, on articulation of student ideas and arguments, and on using representations to justify mathematical ideas. Productive lingering does not mean that teachers stay on an idea and never move forward; it is in the service of moving forward with greater solidity. Lingering means digging into ideas deeply, which requires letting go of assumptions about what students know and understand. In particular, the teachers in these classrooms *don't* assume that:

- because students can do computation involving a particular operation, they've explicitly thought about the operation and how it behaves

- because students have worked with an operation for some years, they don't need to continue digging into the properties and behaviors of the operations, especially as they encounter different kinds of numbers

- once an idea is stated by one student, everyone (or even the student who stated the idea) understands it

- because a student has articulated an idea with advanced mathematical language, that student deeply understands the idea.

These teachers often repeat questions multiple times in the same lesson, insisting that students push harder to think about them, even after some students have offered reasonable responses. The fact that students continue to respond with seriousness and engagement indicates that they don't find the questions tedious or obvious; the ideas are not settled. In fact, over the decade or so in which we have been working closely with teachers to implement these ideas in the classroom, we have been repeatedly struck by how engaging they are to students. As students get used to the kinds of questions teachers ask in these lessons—What do you notice? Why is it happening? Will it work for any numbers? Does the same thing happen with other operations?—they begin to look for structure across problems and make their own conjectures as they deepen their understanding of the operations.

Engaging students in mathematical argument requires a different kind of pace. It requires investigating familiar content in a different way. The lesson sequences on mathematical argument provide a structure for regular work on this key practice. Teachers report that students learn to recognize that making generalizations and constructing arguments is a profound, challenging, and significant part of mathematics, and that they react with excitement when they are able to discover things about mathematics that are seen as interesting and important. In this way, they are learning a set of behaviors that characterize the work of mathematicians.

## CHAPTER FOCUS QUESTIONS

*Use these questions to think back over Chapter 1 as a whole, including the three classroom examples.*

1.  How do the teachers in the classroom examples help students focus on the way an operation behaves *in general*, rather than on calculating answers to individual problems? Identify questions that the teachers in the examples ask that you think are designed to focus students on the operations.

2.  The teachers in the examples often linger on the same question, asking students to restate it or to add their own ideas. Look back at one or two examples of this in the videos. What do you think is gained in terms of student participation? What do you think is gained mathematically?

3.  Do you think this kind of work might be important for your students? Why? What might it offer different students with different combinations of experience, engagement, confidence, and skill in mathematics?

# 2

# Elementary Students as Mathematicians

When students engage in the process of creating mathematical conjectures and arguments, they are behaving like mathematicians. Because most people are unfamiliar with what mathematicians do, one might imagine that they spend their days solving long lists of equations or calculating with very big numbers. But when mathematicians describe their jobs, they are likely to talk about the beauty of the patterns and results they discover, the spirit of curiosity that drives their work, and the satisfaction that comes from using logic to know that something must be true.

While traditional textbooks often start a topic with polished results followed by well-chosen and illustrative exercises for students to try, mathematicians actually begin their investigations by asking questions and playing with examples that may or may not lead to answers. Through these explorations, mathematicians propose, scrutinize, and modify conjectures that describe the patterns that they are noticing. They share their ideas in order to receive feedback, support, and different perspectives. When one of their claims seems sufficiently plausible, they attempt to prove it formally. And it is only when their proof is considered valid by other mathematicians that the theorem (what mathematicians call a proven conjecture) can be published and accepted into the permanent body of mathematical knowledge.

The mathematician's process can be messy, with a great deal of meandering along the journey (complete with side trips and dead ends) from initial questions to final polished results. But it is also full of creativity and surprises, and often "wrong answers" lead to unexpected insights and understanding. This chapter explores the ways that students are functioning like mathematicians (both individually and as a community) when they engage in mathematical argument, as well as the potential benefits and impact of this kind of work. The following investigation will help orient you to the mathematical content of the student discussions, which focus on an aspect of multiplication.

**MATHEMATICAL INVESTIGATION**

Imagine that you hear someone say, "Multiplication makes things bigger." Can you give an example with numbers that would make this statement seem true? Is there a picture that the person might draw to convince you that the claim was always right? What example(s) could you use to show that multiplication doesn't always behave this way?

Now think about different types of numbers that you know. Explore the statement "multiplication makes things bigger" using your number types: Multiply two numbers from the same type or different types, and see how the size of the product compares to the size of the factors. From your analysis, see what kinds of statements you can make about the size of a product relative to the size of the factors you are multiplying.

## THE MATHEMATICIAN'S PROCESS

Even though mathematical research does not follow a clearly defined road map, there are common phases that characterize a typical investigation done by professional mathematicians. The teaching model described in the Introduction also reflects these phases. In this chapter, we will examine these aspects of the process using classroom examples from the lesson sequence, Factors, Products, and Fractions, which includes a study of the statement "multiplication makes bigger."

### Early Questions and Intuition

Mathematicians don't enter their investigations as blank slates. They bring their accumulated mathematical knowledge as well as intuition developed from previous research experiences. This background gives them a sense of what kinds of examples might be fruitful to investigate and helps them formulate their questions and strategies in ways that they hope will be productive. But every exploration is different, and there is no road map to guide the way. Moreover, what appears to be "obvious" in one setting might not even be true in another context. Thus mathematicians learn to test everything and never take their assumptions for granted.

While elementary students may not come into their mathematical investigations with as many years of technical knowledge, they too have acquired skills and intuition that will (and should) influence their entry into a new investigation. In Ms. Laufner's fourth-grade classroom, students are already familiar with multiplication when she casually remarks that this afternoon they will be considering whether multiplication "makes things bigger." Hearing this comment, Danielle nods knowingly and replies, "Yes, because that's what multiplication does. Because, like $3 \times 4$ is 12 and $5 \times 10$ is 50." Overhearing, Amir pipes up, "But $65 \times 1$ is 65!"

When Ms. Laufner brings everyone together for this discussion, she writes the question "Does multiplication always make things bigger?" on poster paper and then calls on Danielle to start.

..................................................................................

**Danielle:** Well, not *always*, but usually.

**Ms. Laufner: Say what you mean.**

**Danielle:** Well, like $2 \times 12$ is 24 and $3 \times 5$ is 15, 24 is bigger and 15 is bigger, so *usually*. But not when you use 1, because then it's the same.

**Ms. Laufner: The same as what?**

**Connor:** It's just the number you were multiplying by.

**Ms. Laufner: Okay, so we have "yes" examples and "no" examples. (*She writes* $2 \times 12 = 24$ *and* $65 \times 1 = 65$ *on the poster paper.*)**

**Alberto:** It would be true if you took out the word *always*. It's the word *always* that is messing that up.

**Ms. Laufner: How would that go?**

**Alberto:** Just, "Does multiplication make things bigger?" And that would be yes, but not always. Also, it wouldn't work with zero.

**Marilyn:** I was just going to say that. Because anything times zero is *zero*.

..................................................................................

Even in this brief and early exchange we see students accessing their prior knowledge to make conjectures. Danielle's original claim that multiplication makes things bigger probably comes from intuition about the whole numbers. Mathematical intuition develops through experience and is essential to mathematicians when they generate and test new ideas in their work. Without these instincts they would simply need to try out case after case algorithmically, without a sense of direction. But they also know that intuition can be deceiving, and sometimes what works in one situation might not be valid in another. So it is never enough to say that a conjecture *looks* true or *seems* obvious—every claim will need to be tested and eventually proven.

### From Examples to Conjectures

It is clear that in Ms. Laufner's classroom examples play an essential role for her students in developing a sense of how something works. This process is not limited to young students—mathematicians also make extensive use of examples. Although the later stages of research do require mathematicians to prove their claims in general rather than just demonstrating them for particular instances, it is a common misconception that doing advanced mathematics means jumping right into the abstract world of variables and formal logic. In fact, concrete examples are fundamental tools for mathematicians in their work.

Mathematicians use examples in many ways. Looking at examples can spark new research questions. For instance, if mathematicians are testing something and every example they try leads to a prime number, they might ask, "Will this *always* produce a prime number?" Or if they stumble upon one example that is different from anything they have ever seen before, mathematicians will ask, "Can we find other examples that also behave in this interesting way?"

Examples can also be used to test existing conjectures. Given a claim about the way something works, mathematicians will check to see if it holds for different examples. These examples help them to build evidence that the conjecture might be true (and hence is worth trying to prove), recognize ways to refine the conjecture if it isn't quite correct, or demonstrate that the conjecture is actually invalid.

When an example is used to show that a claim is not true, it is called a *counterexample*. Counterexamples are incredibly powerful tools for mathematicians—while even a million examples aren't enough to prove that a conjecture is true, a single counterexample is sufficient to show that a conjecture is false.

In the video clips that follow, we see another class of students beginning its investigation of how factor size affects product size in multiplication. In this classroom, the teacher starts the discussion by suggesting that a student might say, "When you multiply, you always get a bigger answer." She first asks students whether they can produce an example that would fit this claim, and only after that does she invite them to comment on whether or not the statement is true.

As you watch these video clips, consider the ways that examples and counterexamples are used and presented, as well as the conjectures that are produced or refuted by the examples.

## FOCUS QUESTIONS

Video 2.1 ▶

http://hein.pub/WDIW2.1

**VIDEO 2.1, SECTION 1** Why might the teacher begin by asking for an example where the claim is true? How does the student show that his example supports the claim?

**VIDEO 2.1, SECTION 2** How does Navea's example show that the claim is not true?

After Navea gives her example verbally, a second student is asked to record it on the board. He writes:

$$1 < 3$$

$$1 \times 3 = 3$$

Has the written work captured Navea's idea? What might you ask next so that the counterexample is clear?

**VIDEO 2.1, SECTION 3** Brage suggests that the only valid counterexample for the claim "When you multiply, you always get a bigger answer" would be $1 \times 1 = 1$. What might his reasoning be?

**VIDEO 2.1, SECTION 4** Naomi suggests that $1 \times 3 = 3$ is an example of an "in between" version of the original conjecture. What does she mean by this? Are there other examples that would support her "in between" conjecture?

**VIDEO 2.1, SECTION 5**   How does Izzie interpret Naomi's "in between" conjecture? Does Gia's example of $0 \times 1 = 0$ fit Izzie's description? Is $0 \times 1 = 0$ a counterexample to the original claim?

.............................................................................................

In the video clips as well as in Ms. Laufner's classroom, we see that the nature of student conjectures is influenced by the examples that the students have produced. In the video, the example $1 \times 3 = 3$ leads to Naomi's proposal that they have an "in between" situation for which the product is bigger than one factor but not bigger than the other. In Ms. Laufner's class, Amir's example of $65 \times 1 = 65$ immediately led Danielle to reconsider her first conjecture.

We see another instance of examples motivating conjectures in the following excerpt, which comes after Ms. Laufner's students have had a chance to turn and talk to a partner for a few moments about whether multiplication makes things bigger.

.............................................................................................

**Danielle:** So, I want to change what I said. Multiplication can never lower itself, and nothing can except subtraction.

**Rohini:** I know what she means. Subtraction is the only one where a number gets lower than itself, because that's take away.

**Mason:** But what about, like, $\frac{1}{2} \times 8$ equals 4?

**Alberto:** I have a conjecture. When you multiply two factors, it's impossible for the product to be lower than both factors. Because, $\frac{1}{2}$ has to get bigger because there are eight groups of it. It can't be lower than itself. Unless it was zero. But then zero would not be lower than itself. In multiplication, the product could be the same as a factor or more than a factor, but not less than both factors.

**Ms. Laufner: Ooh! Let's write this down!**

.............................................................................................

Alberto has produced a new conjecture based on Mason's counterexample to Rohini's claim. Ms. Laufner knows that Alberto's conjecture is not true in all cases, but she writes it down without judgment. She recognizes that what Alberto has proposed fits many of the situations with which her students are currently familiar, and that it is a natural conclusion for the students to make at this point in the conversation. Ms. Laufner knows that as the class continues to investigate the ideas together, they will replace this conjecture with ones that are increasingly precise and mathematically valid.

In fact, later in the class Darya privately shows her teacher a counterexample that she has written down to demonstrate that Alberto's new claim is false: $\frac{2}{6} \times \frac{1}{2} = \frac{1}{6}$. Here Darya is expanding the kinds of examples the class has considered so far to include the product of two numbers between 0 and 1. Based on her equation, Darya has developed a replacement conjecture: "In multiplication, when the first denominator is bigger than the second denominator, the product will be smaller than both factors."

Knowing that most of her students still need time to process the ideas about multiplying a fraction by a whole number, Ms. Laufner chooses not to share Darya's counterexample involving the multiplication of two fractions with the class at this time. She also recognizes that Darya's replacement conjecture is not true, and so she encourages Darya to continue experimenting with more examples on her own.

When mathematicians do research, they don't know what their final results will be, and at every stage their conjectures *seem* plausible based on their current examples. Even though a teacher might know that her students have made a false claim, it is mathematically realistic and worthwhile to record the proposition and then encourage further analysis. Conjectures can also be accepted when they are true for all the situations that the students currently know (such as whole numbers), with the teacher's understanding that they will be revisited later in the year or in a future grade as the students encounter new types of numbers.

### Restricting and Generalizing

Mathematicians love to find theorems about the most general situations they can, but large-scale claims are not always accessible or true. And even when a conjecture is ostensibly correct, a valid proof can be elusive to find. As a result, mathematicians frequently break their questions into more manageable pieces and initially consider their conjectures in limited contexts.

Danielle originally proposed a sweeping conjecture—that multiplication *always* makes things bigger. If a mathematician were to state this formally, it might look like this: "Given any two numbers $x$ and $y$, the product $xy$ is greater than both $x$ and $y$." It would be powerful if we could characterize the behavior of multiplication in such a universal theorem that was true for any numbers that we encountered—whole numbers, fractions, negative numbers, and so on. But as Ms. Laufner's students realize, the size of the product isn't bigger than its factors in all cases.

Just like the students, mathematicians often find that they have to break things down into smaller pieces when deciding when a conjecture might be valid. One way that mathematicians limit the scope of a conjecture is by considering what are called *special cases*. Although a counterexample might show that a proposed conjecture is false, this does not always mean that the entire claim should be thrown out. Sometimes that example is best treated as a special case that behaves differently than most other instances and can be separated off from an otherwise true theorem. For example, if someone claimed that all prime numbers were odd, that would be false. But rather than abandoning the conjecture, mathematicians could treat 2 as a special case and declare instead that all prime numbers *except* 2 are odd. Notice how this response is fundamentally different from how we would react to the counterexample $5 - 7 \neq 7 - 5$ for a claim that subtraction is commutative. In that case we would reject the entire conjecture as faulty, because $5 - 7$ is not an isolated example.

In our classroom examples, students invoke familiar special cases such as 0 and 1. Introducing students directly to the notion of special cases can help them articulate stronger and more precise conjectures by allowing them to incorporate these exceptions explicitly into their claims, rather than using vague terms like *usually* or *not always*.

Of course, mathematicians can't always fix a conjecture by throwing out one or a few special cases. A conjecture might not be true for every number on the number line (what mathematicians would call the *real numbers*), but it might be true for a large subset of those numbers, such as all the positive numbers or all the even integers.

Mathematicians often state their claims in the form of an "if-then" statement, where the "if" part is called the *hypothesis* and the "then" part is called the *conclusion*. (Note that this use of the word *hypothesis* is different from the way it is generally used in the context of science, where the hypothesis refers to a conjectured outcome, relationship, or explanation.) For instance, in the statement "If an integer is a multiple of 6, then it is even," the hypothesis is *an integer is a multiple of 6* and the conclusion is *it is even*. So if mathematicians observe something about a particular category of numbers, they may *restrict* their conjecture to that category (like multiples of 6) by putting it into the hypothesis of their conjecture.

It is worth noting that a conjecture can be true even if it is not stated for the largest possible category of numbers. The statement "If an integer is a multiple of 6, then it is even" is true, despite the fact that the hypothesis could be expanded to include multiples of any even number. An if-then statement is true as long as the conclusion holds whenever the hypothesis holds. Students often produce conjectures like this that are more restrictive than they could be, but this does not mean the claims are untrue or that they must be expanded in order to be validated. Also, students do not have to use the formal language or structure of an if-then statement—even professional mathematicians have many different ways of expressing their theorems.

Ms. Laufner's students recognized quickly that their original conjecture wasn't true for all numbers. In this next excerpt, the students revise that conjecture by restricting it to a familiar category of numbers.

.................................................................................................

**Ms. Laufner:** When you thought that multiplication always made numbers bigger, you were thinking about just certain kinds of numbers, and for those numbers, you were right. Do you know what kinds of numbers you were thinking about? Because it's important.

**Danielle:** Regular numbers.

**Ms. Laufner:** Yes! There's another name for those numbers . . .

**Alberto:** Whole numbers?

**Ms. Laufner:** Yes! So if our conjecture had read, "Multiplying whole numbers . . ."

**Alberto:** Not counting 1!

**Ms. Laufner:** "Greater than 1, always make things bigger" What would you all say to that?

**Class:** Yes!

**Ms. Laufner:** And a whole number times a fraction . . .

**Class:** Less than the number you started with.

.................................................................................................

Although this is still a bit imprecise (and not true for fractions greater than 1, such as $\frac{3}{2}$), the students have begun to hone the class of numbers to include in their ultimate conjectures. The next video highlights another example of a restricted conjecture, in which the equation $6 \times \frac{1}{2} = 3$ leads Brage to postulate about the behavior of multiplication for a very specific subset of numbers.

**I** FOCUS QUESTIONS **I**

**VIDEO 2.2**   What conjecture does Brage extrapolate from the example $6 \times \frac{1}{2} = 3$? How is he restricting his conjecture to a smaller set of numbers? Is Brage's conjecture true?

What examples might students provide to support this conjecture? What other examples could they try to see if the restrictions in the conjecture could be expanded?

http://hein.pub/WDIW2.2

The restrictions that students put on their conjectures will often emerge from the examples that they have produced. In the video, Brage treats $\frac{1}{2}$ as a special case and restricts the other set of factors to even whole numbers. Students should be allowed to investigate situations that arise naturally for them, expanding their explorations slowly, and not be rushed to a generalization that is outside their current scope of vision. For instance, Brage's classmates might next try multiplying $\frac{1}{2}$ by an odd number or replacing $\frac{1}{2}$ with another familiar fraction.

### Constructing Proofs

Once mathematicians have accumulated significant evidence that a conjecture is true, they need to write a proof to turn the conjecture into a theorem. Without a proof, it is possible that 999,999 examples will work, but the millionth one won't. A proof is a formal argument using established rules of logic, definitions, axioms, and already proven theorems to demonstrate that a claim *must* be true. Once a proof exists it means that mathematicians can stop testing examples or worrying that their intuition has led them to believe something that will later turn out to be wrong.

Elementary students do not generally use the abstract logic or technical notation of professional mathematicians, but they can learn to distinguish between noticing a feature of a collection of examples and assuming that characteristic will be present all the time. Moreover, they can begin to understand that an argument *must* be provided to justify a general conjecture, and that even lots of examples (or one really big example) isn't enough to show that a claim is always true.

In much the same way as professional mathematicians use definitions and axioms in their proofs, elementary students use representations as a basis for their arguments. When engaging in mathematical argument, student mathematicians spend a lot of time developing these representations, analyzing them, and connecting them to their class conjectures (as we discussed in Chapter 1).

In each of the classrooms visited so far in this chapter, we have seen that the student discussion eventually included fractions. This investigation led one class to produce the following conjecture (note that although it's not explicitly stated, they were considering only positive fractions):

*If you multiply a whole number greater than 1 by a fraction less than 1, then the product will be bigger than the fraction and less than the whole number.*

In our next video, the class has been developing representations for a particular instance of this conjecture using the following story context:

*Joey runs $\frac{3}{4}$ of a mile each day for 12 days. How many miles does Joey run in all?*

Before watching the video, try the mathematical investigation on your own.

## MATHEMATICAL INVESTIGATION

What equation would model the story context given above? Come up with a visual representation of your equation. Notice where you see each of the factors, the product, and the operation of multiplication in your representation.

In what ways could your representation be used to support the claim that multiplying a whole number greater than 1 by a positive fraction less than 1 results in a product that is bigger than the fraction and less than the whole number?

## ▌ FOCUS QUESTIONS ▐

**VIDEO 2.3** What aspects of Jay and Harry's representation does this discussion clarify for students?

Video 2.3 ▶

http://hein.pub/WDIW2.3

What is important about the fact that Jay and Harry have combined their quarter circles to make 9 whole circles, rather than just drawing 12 separate circles with 3 quarters of each shaded in? How does this connect the representation to the class conjecture?

....................

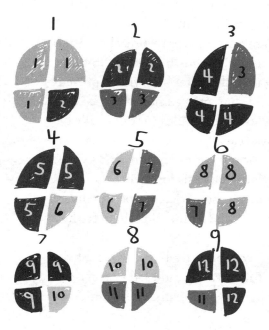

In the video, we see the students carefully analyzing all the aspects of this visual representation.

At first, some students struggle to connect the picture to the story and are confused by the different meaning of numbers inside and outside of the circles. But as the discussion progresses, students audibly react as they begin to understand the representation and can identify where they see both days and miles in the drawing. They also observe that since three quarters fill less than a whole circle, a fourth quarter (in a new color) from the next day has to be used to complete the circle and make up a whole mile.

Although this class discussion doesn't include a general justification for the conjecture, the seeds of a representation-based argument are being laid here. By noticing that each colored set of three quarters is less than a full circle, the students start to see why pushing together 12 copies of $\frac{3}{4}$ will result in fewer than 12 full circles (and thus why $12 \times \frac{3}{4}$ is less than 12). Students can also recognize that 12 copies of $\frac{3}{4}$ is more than one copy of $\frac{3}{4}$, so the product of 12 (the whole number) and $\frac{3}{4}$ (the fraction less than 1) must be bigger than the fraction factor.

Not every class needs to end at a completely general argument, but representations can be explored to see how they might be adapted to other examples of the conjecture and whether they could be used to show that the conjecture would be true for *any* example. If the teacher in the video wanted her students to work toward a generalization, she might have them look next at other whole-number multiples of $\frac{3}{4}$ or look at 12 copies of a different fraction, like $\frac{2}{3}$ or $\frac{1}{2}$.

### Sharing Results and Motivating Future Research

Just like the students in our episodes, mathematicians brainstorm and share their work with each other at all stages of progress. When mathematicians believe they have written a proof for a conjecture, they let other mathematicians read it to make sure that it is understandable and doesn't contain mathematical errors. They also present their work at conferences, where people can ask questions and make suggestions. This promotes a collective responsibility that ensures theorems have logically valid arguments to back them up, since future mathematics will be built off of their foundation. Once these proofs have been verified and polished, the theorems can be published in journals and textbooks, where they will inspire mathematicians to ask new questions and continue the research cycle.

In the previous video, students were vocal about the ways in which they came to interpret and ultimately appreciate the representation. While it is a worthwhile ideal to have every student understand and approve of the work done by the class, there is likely to be a variety of levels of understanding at the end of an investigation, and not every group will be able to reach a unified position. Sometimes a student is still confused or simply unconvinced, even after most students are on board and the class has spent significant periods of time working through these matters. In these instances, the teacher should encourage students to continue thinking about the ideas and may wish to leave open the possibility that the class will return to the discussion if something new comes to light.

It is quite common for professional mathematicians to leave an open conjecture on the table when a proof cannot be found. And even when a proof is discovered, it can contain complex ideas that may take other mathematicians a long time to understand. Elementary student mathematicians can be reassured that there is no implication an individual student (or the process) has failed if there isn't complete agreement and closure at the point where a teacher feels that the group needs to move forward. The students will have deepened their conceptual understanding through the process of engaging in mathematical argument, even if the status of some conjectures is left open at the end of the discussion or lesson sequence.

## FACILITATING A COMMUNITY OF STUDENT MATHEMATICIANS

Most research work done by professional mathematicians is self-directed. They find questions that interest them and pursue the answers using their knowledge and intuition. Elementary student mathematicians have an influential voice in the direction and content of their work, but their teacher plays a unique and integral role in these endeavors. As the facilitator of a community of mathematicians, the teacher needs to share mathematical authority with her students in a genuine way. At the same time, she holds a position of leadership, and both her mathematical knowledge and pedagogical skills are essential for guiding the class in a responsible and productive manner. In sharing mathematical authority, a teacher must be open to the prospect of following students' thoughts as they unfold, knowing that sometimes these ideas could lead to a faulty conjecture or a winding route to the expected destination. Earlier in this section we saw Ms. Laufner enthusiastically respond to Alberto's conjecture that multiplication can never result in a product that is less than both factors, despite recognizing the mathematical problems with his claim. And in one of the videos, we watched students being allowed to spend time discussing a highly specific conjecture about multiplying even whole numbers by the fraction $\frac{1}{2}$, rather than being directed to consider bigger sets or broader generalizations.

At the same time, the teacher knows the overarching agenda of the lesson sequence and understands the mathematical concepts involved. This knowledge and foresight can be used to help her decide when to have the whole class follow a student's suggestion and when it would be better to "park" an idea. The teacher also uses her judgment about whether to share an example or ask a question about an idea that students might not produce on their own. Ms. Laufner decided not to present a counterexample to Alberto's conjecture (such as $\frac{1}{2} \times \frac{1}{2} = \frac{1}{4}$) because it felt like it would unnaturally force her students into an area that they weren't ready to discuss yet. At other times, though, it can be helpful for the teacher to bring in a new idea that helps students to move forward. In the video classroom we visited earlier, some students come to think that Brage's conjecture is true only for even whole numbers being multiplied by $\frac{1}{2}$, and it is the teacher who encourages them to investigate what happens when they use an odd whole number instead.

In the next two video clips, we see a teacher making choices in the moment about how to respond to student suggestions, especially ones that are unexpected. In the first clip, a student has just conjectured that if you want the product to be bigger than the factors in multiplication, your factors must be at least 2.

| FOCUS QUESTIONS |

**VIDEO 2.4**   Why might the teacher have decided to postpone a discussion of Katrina's conjecture that $2 \times 2 = 4$ is the "smallest" example in which the product is bigger than both factors? Why does she choose not to have the class investigate the examples with negative numbers?

Video 2.4 ▶

http://hein.pub/WDIW2.4

The teacher puts a box around the equation $2 \times 2 = 4$ and indicates that this will be a great starting point for considering Katrina's conjecture. But she explains that they haven't fully explored the situation yet, so she's going to wait before having the class focus on making arguments about the claim.

As she is writing, though, a few students begin to wonder about examples with negative numbers $2 \times -1$. The teacher endorses these questions as worthwhile and promises that it's something they can revisit in the future, but she notes that she is delaying a discussion in which not everyone would be able to participate, because the class hasn't yet learned to multiply with negative numbers.

The second clip arises in the same class, but a few minutes later. The class has been recapping where they stand on the question, "Does multiplication always make things bigger?" Many students point out that the answer is "no" because of the word *always*. But one student suggests that if a change were made to the wording of the question, the answer could actually be "yes." Wanting to encourage everyone to be involved in developing these ideas, the teacher asks if another student can say what this new question might be.

## ▌ FOCUS QUESTIONS

Video
2.5 ▶

http://hein.pub/WDIW2.5

**VIDEO 2.5**　Megan's response changes the question (informally) to "Does multiplication make things bigger than addition?" Do you think that this was what the original student was thinking about when he suggested changing the question? What might his question have been?

How does the teacher respond to Megan's idea? What decisions might she need to make next in leading the discussion?

It is evident in these videos that the teacher facilitates the conversations in such a way that students are talking to each other and building off one another's ideas, promoting a sense of collective ownership. When sharing mathematical authority in the classroom, the teacher encourages students to turn to their peers when seeking clarification, insight, or validation. The articulation of the conjectures and arguments comes primarily from the students, and ultimately students will have a say in determining whether those arguments are convincing.

When the teacher does assert a more directive leadership position and puts an idea to the side, she explains her decision and maintains a spirit of collaboration between herself and the students. If a student's suggestion will take the discussion in a tangential direction, as Megan's does in the video, the teacher can choose whether it is reasonable to follow that digression for a period of time or whether to encourage interested students to investigate the idea on their own later. In all of these ways the teacher makes it clear that she is not the exclusive arbiter of correctness and that students have agency in the development of the mathematics.

## WHY SHOULD STUDENTS ACT LIKE MATHEMATICIANS?

When students read and write stories, they have the opportunity to become immersed in the characters and the plot. They visualize themselves inside the narrative and want to fully understand the characters' experiences, whether as a reader or an author. Students know that they will never run out of books to read, that there are all different genres to match their interests, and that they have the ability to write stories of their own. They learn that creative writing starts with a rough draft that gets better as a result of being shared and revised into a final version. They understand that editing is simply part of the process, and it doesn't mean that the first draft was wrong or bad.

Too often, this is the opposite of students' experiences with mathematics. For students to be drawn to engage in mathematics, it is essential that they encounter the subject as a creative field in which they can play an integral role. They should have images of mathematicians as curious and imaginative people who love doing mathematics but who still make mistakes and get stuck on hard problems.

It is exciting for professional mathematicians to realize that their own discoveries can contribute to the ever-growing body of mathematical knowledge. When elementary students have the opportunity to create mathematics that is *brand-new to them*, participating in the act of innovation can empower them. As students start to make their own conjectures and arguments, the goal of mathematics ceases to be about providing correct answers to someone else's questions. Instead, mathematics becomes focused on the creative process and the search for understanding. Moreover, mathematical work doesn't end when answers are found, because those answers help to inspire new questions.

The practice of functioning as mathematicians is about more than just making math more engaging and fun for students. The process that mathematicians work through in their research increases their depth of understanding. By precisely articulating claims, testing them with examples, and seeking logical proofs, mathematicians clarify meaning, illuminate misconceptions, and ensure that their final results are incontrovertible. In emulating this process, students learn that there is value in exploring *why* an answer is correct and recognize that representations can be more than just illustrations of a calculation. They learn that so-called wrong answers often shed light on what the right approach will be and might spark alternative investigations. By framing the work in this spirit, students are given an authentic purpose for sharing a response that is not quite correct or still in a garbled form.

Engaging in mathematics like a mathematician also more naturally mirrors the way that people discover and understand new ideas. In the early stages of a research investigation, even the *questions* might not be completely clear, never mind a way to find the answers. Too often we hear students say in math class that they don't want to speak up because they are "still thinking" or they don't want to give answers they aren't sure are correct. It is helpful for students to know that a fundamental characteristic of professional mathematicians is the willingness to try out ideas without prejudice and to share work that might be wrong.

Moreover, emphasizing the fact that students form a *community* of mathematicians places value on every contribution. Students come to see that everyone has a role to play, and that even small contributions, like asking a question, giving a partial answer, noticing a counterexample or special case, proposing a change in phrasing, or drawing a clear representation, can have an impact on the community's success.

Mathematicians know that good conjectures are characterized not just by the truthfulness of their content but also by their clarity, precision, and understandability. The students want their conjectures and arguments to reflect their intended meaning in a way that would be comprehensible to someone else from outside their community, such as a student from another classroom. It is an essential part of the process for students to contribute a variety of approaches and suggestions and to be proactive about asking questions and responding to other students' ideas throughout the phases of work. Respectful critiquing of mathematical claims becomes a natural and essential step toward creating the best class conjecture and argument. In viewing themselves and their peers as collaborating mathematicians, students can feel safe (and have mathematical purpose in) admitting that they disagree with a friend or don't fully comprehend someone else's idea.

A classroom of student mathematicians is one in which everyone engages in the content of the work, collaborates to produce community results, and is self-reflective about their own understanding. As members of a mathematical community, students gain confidence in their own voice as mathematicians and value the knowledge and contributions of their peers. Ultimately, the experience of behaving and perceiving themselves as mathematicians has the power to radically alter what students believe about the nature of mathematics and the role that they can play in the subject itself.

## CHAPTER FOCUS QUESTIONS

*Use these questions to think back over Chapter 2 as a whole, including the classroom examples and video clips.*

1.  **How can encouraging students to act like mathematicians affect their participation in class discussions? In what ways did students in the classroom examples function both individually and as a community of mathematicians?**

2.  **In a classroom community, the teacher shares mathematical authority with students but still has a key role to play in guiding the work. What mathematical situations arose in the classroom episodes where a teacher needed to make a key decision about how to respond? Are there instances where a different teacher response might have taken the class in an alternative mathematical direction? What factors might you use in choosing your own response to these situations?**

3.  **Considering your own classroom teaching, are there ways that you could incorporate aspects of the mathematician's process into other mathematics lessons?**

# 3

# The Teaching Model

This chapter provides an overview of a teaching model for implementing mathematical argument in the classroom, illustrated by examples from classrooms using the lesson sequence, Changing a Number in Addition or Multiplication (see pages 130–156 for the complete sequence). This sequence includes work on a generalization about addition—*when one addend of an addition expression is increased by some amount and the other addend stays the same, the sum increases by that same amount*—followed by looking at what happens in an analogous situation with a contrasting operation, in this case, multiplication. You worked on the addition generalization in the first mathematical investigation in Chapter 1.

In this chapter, the examples focus on student thinking and discourse to give you images of the kind of learning students do in each phase of the model. In Chapter 4, we'll examine each phase again, with an eye toward how teachers support student learning.

The teaching model comprises five phases:

- Phase I: Noticing regularity. Students examine pairs or sequences of related problems, equations, or expressions and describe patterns they notice.

- Phase II: Articulating a claim. Based on the patterns noticed in Phase I, students work individually and collectively to write a conjecture clearly enough so that someone not in the class could understand it.

- Phase III: Investigating through representations. Students represent specific instances of the claim with manipulatives, diagrams, or story contexts.

- Phase IV: Constructing arguments. Students use representations to explain why the conjecture must be true for all numbers of a certain class (e.g., all whole numbers, all positive rational numbers, etc.).

- Phase V: Comparing operations. Once students have verified a claim, they consider the question, Does this work for other operations? Returning to Phase I, students consider a set of problems, equations, or expressions that illustrate an analogous claim for another operation. They then go on to Phases II through IV to examine and prove a conjecture about the second operation.

Although these phases might be considered stages of an investigation, they are not necessarily distinct and don't necessarily follow exactly in this order. As illustrated in Chapter 1, students might work with representations as they engage in noticing or in articulating a claim. Or they might contrast operations before they construct arguments that explain why the different generalizations must be true. However, these five phases constitute the essential aspects of mathematical argument and are the skeleton upon which the lesson sequences are built.

## INTRODUCING THE LESSON SEQUENCE

Video 3.1 ▶

http://hein.pub/WDIW3.1

Before we examine the five phases of the teaching model, consider one teacher's introduction of this sequence to her fourth-grade class.

The teacher tells her students they will be doing a series of short sessions in which they'll think together about things they can say about addition and multiplication—ways in which the operations are the same and how they are different. To mark these sessions as separate from their regular math class, the class will refer to them as Algebra and Proof sessions (other teachers have used other names such as Making and Proving Conjectures or Mathematical Argument). The teacher explains that during these sessions, they will look for things they can say that are generally true about an operation, state their conjectures clearly using precise language, and work together to prove their conjectures. This teacher is defining for her students an aspect of algebra—articulating and proving generalizations about the operations—that is often hidden from students in introductory algebra courses. Such an orientation will serve students both now and in those later courses. By associating the work of these sequences with the words *algebra* and *proof*, students will meet those words with the expectation that the corresponding content is engaging and accessible. Naming the lessons in this way both helps with establishing continuity between sessions and sets up students' expectations that the work they will be doing is important and advanced.

In the rest of the chapter, we trace a class engaging in the five phases of the mathematical-argument-teaching model. The example we use in the text of the chapter is a composite, based on several of our collaborating classrooms; we've given this teacher the name Audrey Kent. The examples in the text as well as additional video examples are from second-, third-, and fourth-grade classrooms in which students were working on one or both of these generalizations.

## PHASE I: NOTICING REGULARITY

*Students examine pairs or sequences of related problems, equations, or expressions and describe patterns they notice.*

Many elementary students spontaneously notice generalizations about the behavior of the operations and sometimes remark on them in surprise: "Hey, when we found combinations of 7, every combination has an opposite! Like $3 + 4$ and $4 + 3$. The same thing happened when we did combinations of 6." Some students may not explicitly state a generalization, but one can find it implicit in their work. The first grader who writes, "I know $5 + 5 = 10$, so $5 + 6 = 11$," seems to recognize that when 1 is added to an addend, the sum increases by 1. However, many students have not developed the habit of looking for such regularity. For example, consider how Ms. Kent began the sequence with this poster.

| | |
|---|---|
| $7 + 5 = 12$ <br> $7 + 6 = \underline{\quad}$ | $7 + 5 = 12$ <br> $8 + 5 = \underline{\quad}$ |
| $9 + 4 = 13$ <br> $9 + 5 = \underline{\quad}$ | $9 + 4 = 13$ <br> $10 + 4 = \underline{\quad}$ |

**What do you notice?**

**What's happening here?**

Ms. Kent acknowledged to her students that the numbers were not challenging, emphasizing that the purpose of the discussion was to consider what is happening in the pairs of problems and to state ideas clearly and convincingly. The class filled in the blanks and then talked about what they noticed. Students mentioned that, in moving from the first to second equation in each pair, one number changed, one stayed the same, and the last number in the equation changed, too. The discussion went on for a few minutes, until Frank, said, "Since $9 + 4$ is 13, $9 + 5$ *has* to be 1 more than 13."

The initial response of the class is common: Students looked at specific numbers without thinking about the changes *in relation* to each other. Frank, on the other hand, asserted that 13 must increase to 14 *because* 4 increased to 5. He saw how those changes must happen together.

Ms. Kent recognized the importance of Frank's statement and his assertion of necessity and asked the class to break into pairs to discuss it. When the class came back together, more students were able to describe how a change in one addend of an addition expression is related to a change in the sum. Partway through the discussion, Rose said, "I was just wondering. How did Frank come up with the idea he had? Because these are not just everyday ideas that you come up with every day."

Frank responded, "I'm not really sure. I just know it. It kind of seems obvious to me, so I didn't think to think about it before."

For Rose, noticing patterns in the number system was a new and important kind of mathematical activity, while, for Frank, some generalizations are so obvious as to be invisible. Most classrooms are likely to include students like Frank, who made use of the pattern without explicitly thinking about it, as well as students like Rose, who have never looked for such patterns before.

Whether an individual student is for the first time finding patterns in the number system, finding language to describe the pattern he or she has noticed, or beginning to articulate the mathematical relationships that underlie the pattern, all students in the class are engaged in the same discussion. The entire class benefits from the range of questions and ideas, although each student may be learning something different.

Because most students have not experienced focused discussion of such generalizations, first, we need to cultivate in the class the habit of looking for and expressing regularity. Presenting to students sets of problems that embody the relationship to be explored is one way to start this cultivation.

.........................................................................................

Video from a fourth-grade class illustrates how another teacher approached the first session of this sequence. In order to begin the investigation, the teacher presented the class with the following pairs of equations:

$$12 + 8 = 20$$
$$12 + 10 = 22$$

––––––––––––––––––

$$38 + 45 = 83$$
$$38 + 50 = 88$$

## FOCUS QUESTIONS

Video 3.2 ▶

http://hein.pub/WDIW3.2

**VIDEO 3.2, SECTION 1** How does the teacher help students attend to the precision of their language so they can communicate more clearly?

**VIDEO 3.2, SECTION 2** Arden begins the discussion by pointing out that in one pair of equations, the sums differ by 2, and in the other pair, the sums differ by 5. It is common for students to first look at specific changes in an equation without noticing how numbers change in relation to each other. How does Isaac talk about the change in the sum as related to the change in addends? What does Maddie's statement add to Isaac's?

**VIDEO 3.2, SECTION 3** Amina and Jasper have offered another pair of equations. In what ways are their new equations another example of the same pattern illustrated by the first two pairs? What are differences about the new pair that would be important to discuss as a class?

**VIDEO 3.2, SECTION 4**   When students notice a pattern, why is it insufficient for them to say, "It works"? What is gained as students try to describe the pattern more precisely? What is useful about having students write individually rather than continue orally as a group? Why would the teacher ask students to do this writing as the concluding activity for the day?

..................................................................................

Students begin their work on mathematical argument by looking for patterns in sets of related problems. These problems are examples of the generalization they will be working on in the next phases. Noticing patterns and regularities, whether by young students or professional mathematicians, is an essential part of doing mathematics. This beginning phase of exploration results in observations that can lead to identification and elaboration of important mathematical ideas. Through classroom interaction, sometimes in pairs and small groups but largely in whole-class discussion, students elaborate their own thinking and engage with their classmates' ideas. As they look across multiple examples, students notice and describe the common underlying structure. Some students may begin to articulate their ideas about the mathematical relationships they are noticing, anticipating the work the class will do next in Phase II.

## PHASE II: ARTICULATING A CLAIM

*Based on the patterns the students noticed in Phase I, they work individually and collectively to write a conjecture clear enough that someone not in the class could understand it.*

Noticing regularity leads to a claim that a relationship holds for a set of expressions or equations. During Phase I, students are often already beginning to try to state the relationship they are noticing. In this second phase, as students work together as a class to articulate their ideas clearly, they also clarify for themselves exactly what it is they noticed in the examples they examined.

Frequently, this aspect of the sequence begins with students working individually to state a claim. Some students, particularly those who struggle with language, may list additional examples that embody the same relationship. Others use words to state the claim. While it is helpful to the class to list a range of numerical examples, and this contribution should be acknowledged, the main work of this phase is to devise a statement with words.

After the students work individually, the teacher selects several individuals' statements that contain elements the class may want to draw on as they work together to create a "class conjecture." The teacher may also select statements (or make up statements) that include errors or ambiguities that are important to bring to the class' attention.

Returning to our example: Ms. Kent began the next lesson about adding 1 to an addend by posting additional numerical examples listed by her students along with the following student statements:

- In the first column, if the number goes up, the answer goes up.

- The first number goes up by 1 and the second number stays the same, so the last number goes up by 1.

- One number grows by 1, so the sum grows by 1.

An essential aspect of articulating a claim is figuring out which elements are key to expressing the relationship illustrated by the examples. This determination involves coordinating the changing elements and figuring out what is at the root of the relationship. In the previous examples, the student have identified the following important elements in one, two, or all of their statements:

- Two numbers increase.

- Two numbers increase by 1.

- One number stays the same.

- One of the numbers that increases is the sum.

As students work together to articulate a class conjecture, they consider the choice of words, the extent of precision, and which components are relevant. When students state their ideas, it is important that they use language that is meaningful to them. The teacher may also introduce technical vocabulary and symbols as the need arises, especially to clarify referents. For example, if students use the word *number* to refer to different objects in their claim, the teacher might ask students how someone reading their words will know what they're referring to. She might also suggest such terms as *addend* or *sum* so that students hear more precise language and begin to use it themselves. This introduction of mathematical terms can also help draw students' attention to the operation they are considering.

If the class composes a version of the conjecture with technical vocabulary that is new to some students, it is also useful to present a version with more familiar vocabulary. Having both versions posted throughout the sequence helps students stay connected to the idea while also helping them become more familiar and fluent with technical vocabulary.

Throughout the discussion, students work to understand each other's articulations. A statement that may seem clear to the teacher may not be clear to the class, and so the teacher can ask individual students to paraphrase the statement of another. Students might suggest alternative wording or ask each other questions to clarify. They can point to specific referents of the terms on a list of numerical examples or check their statements against those examples. As questions arise, students might create new examples to test the limits or extent of their conjecture.

By the end of Ms. Kent's lesson, the class agreed on the following statement as their conjecture:

*In addition, if you increase one of the addends by 1 and keep the other addend the same, then the sum will also increase by 1.*

Only one of the initial statements they considered as a class included a specific reference to addition ("One number grows by 1, so the sum grows by 1"). As students discussed their statements, they incorporated language that made it clear that they are talking about addition, although they still may not realize that this characteristic is specific only to that operation.

...........................................................

The following video shows another example of a class in the process of articulating a conjecture. In this case, the fourth graders are considering not just what happens when 1 is added to an addend but what happens when *any number* is added to an addend. The teacher presents the statements of two students for the class to consider. As you watch this video, consider the language students use to convey generality.

## ▌ FOCUS QUESTIONS ▐

**VIDEO 3.3** In what ways are the conjectures stated in the video clip more general than those of Ms. Kent's students? What language do the students use to convey generality? In what ways have students chosen language with precision?

Video 3.3 ▶

http://hein.pub/WDIW3.3

...........................................................

The task of articulating a general claim is challenging and engaging and serves the range of students. The relationship the class is exploring is new to many students, and the effort to find language for their ideas solidifies their understanding. As they work to articulate the claim, they may frequently return to specific numbers to clarify the relationship for themselves. For students who already have a strong sense of the relationship, the challenge is to find language to describe it precisely. These students might also return to specific numbers to communicate more clearly what the referents are. Once a claim has been articulated, having students connect the components of the claim to the class' examples further supports understanding for all students.

Even after a generalization has been stated, the class might linger on the idea as students continue to challenge themselves to say it in their own words. Each new formulation offers a new slant, illuminates nuances, or solidifies the idea, both for the student making the statement and for the other students who are listening. They consider different ways of communicating the generalization with precision, thinking about whether their statements have captured the key mathematical features of their conjecture and how their words might be interpreted by someone outside their class who had not been participating in their discussion. As students linger on the details of the articulation, they deepen their thinking about the mathematics involved in their conjecture and learn about the mathematical process of constructing and communicating mathematical claims.

# PHASE III: INVESTIGATING THROUGH REPRESENTATIONS

*Students represent specific instances of the claim with manipulatives, diagrams, or story contexts.*

In the elementary grades, representations in the form of physical models, drawings, diagrams, number lines, arrays, and story contexts are tools for thinking, communicating, and constructing arguments. Representations that embody the relationships defined by the operations allow students to examine *why* the symbol patterns they identified work. They help students develop their own internal logic and connect the words of their conjecture to images of the operation and to its symbolic representation.

Students may work individually or in pairs to create a representation that illustrates the relationships in the generalization they are exploring. After students have completed their representations, the teacher selects a set of them to discuss in class. The set should illustrate a variety of representations, thus building a repertoire students can use to understand the operations.

It is the responsibility of the class to critique each student representation. Students state what they understand in the representation and ask questions about what they don't understand.

For example, Ms. Kent presented the following story problem to her class:

*Nomi found 4 rocks and Alec found 6. How many rocks did they find?*

*On the way home, Alec found 1 more rock. Now Nomi has 4 rocks and Alec has 7. How many rocks did they find?*

She asked students to create representations to show *why* the sum, 4 + 7, must be 1 more than the sum of 4 + 6. When the students came together to share their representations, Ms. Kent prompted the discussion by asking a set of questions for each representation.

- Where do you see 4 and 6?

- Where do you see 10?

- How is addition represented?

- Where do you see the 1 that was added to 6?

- How does your representation show the sum increased by 1?

This set of questions is an example of what we call core questions, which are included in all of the lesson sequences. Designed to connect the representations and elements of the claim, the questions emphasize how the operation is shown. That is, they shift attention from an exclusive focus on quantities to include the action or the relationships defined by the operation. Although these core questions may seem straightforward, we have found that they take students into deeper understanding of the representation and often uncover confusions the class needs to work through about the mathematical relationships they are attempting to represent.

In Ms. Kent's class, Darren offered the following drawing as a representation of 4 + 6 and 4 + 7. However, his classmates could not find 4 + 6 in the representation, even after he tried to show them several times how he saw the quantity of 6 embedded in the quantity of 7.

Although Ms. Kent understood Darren's explanation, she decided it would be helpful to discuss several of the other representations before returning to Darren's. Natalie showed her representation using cubes.

Ms. Kent asked some core questions. "How does Natalie's representation show 4 + 6, the rocks that Nomi and Alec found at first? Where is the sum of 4 + 6? What about the second part of the story—how does this representation show the 6 changing to a 7 and the 10 changing to 11?" Karim explained that 4 + 6 is shown in Natalie's representation by the white and pink cubes, and 10 is the total

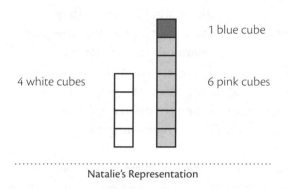

Natalie's Representation

1 blue cube

4 white cubes        6 pink cubes

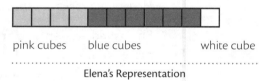

Darren's Representation

of those two stacks. He covered up the blue cube with his hand and pushed the two stacks together to show the sum of 6 and 4. He then revealed the blue cube, explaining that by adding that cube, 4 + 6 is transformed to 4 + 7, and the total becomes 11. The blue cube indicates both that one addend increased from 6 to 7 and that the sum increased from 10 to 11.

The class also looked at Elena's cube representation, represented by this drawing, and compared it to Natalie's.

pink cubes        blue cubes        white cube

Elena's Representation

Before continuing to read about the class' discussion, pause here to consider for yourself what you see in each of the student representations. What differences do you see among Darren's, Natalie's, and Elena's representations? How does each show the original addends, the change in an addend, the original sum, and the change in the sum? What might students get out of each of the representations, and what might they get by comparing them?

Through such comparisons, students make explicit which aspects of the representations reveal the mathematical structure (the quantities represented and how they are related) and which are incidental (in this case, the colors of the cubes and their relative positions). In comparing Natalie's and Elena's cube stacks, Paul said, "They're kind of the same, but Natalie's isn't stuck together like Elena's." When Ms. Kent asked what Paul might mean by "they're kind of the same," Deana said, "They're both showing how you add 1 more." At this point, Gordon said, "Wait a minute. That's like what Darren had." Gordon held Natalie's white stack against Darren's drawing of 4 squares and her pink-and-blue stack over the drawing of 7 squares. The cube representation gave clarity to Darren's drawing so that Gordon could show the class how 4 + 6 was embedded in Darren's representation of 4 + 7. Although Darren himself had been clear about this all along, it had been hidden for many of the other students.

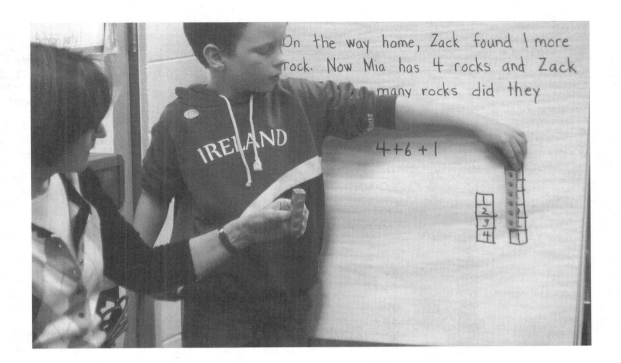

These students were learning to compare representations to look for correspondences across them. In this case, the comparison helped the class interpret a representation that originally stymied them. Ms. Kent concluded the discussion by suggesting their new insights about Darren's representation could help them interpret drawings in the future. When they see their classmates' drawings, they might imagine cubes and think about how the cubes can be broken apart, moved around, or shown in different colors. When they create a drawing, they might think about what to include to help others interpret it.

Different representations may make different features of the mathematics more obvious, or students may find that certain representations connect more clearly to their own understanding than others. Through considering representations different from their own, students come to identify and describe the salient features and structure of the mathematical relationships they are investigating. By seeing the same idea represented in different forms, students develop a deeper understanding of the mathematical abstractions embodied in their conjecture.

## PHASE IV: CONSTRUCTING ARGUMENTS

*Students use representations to explain why the conjecture must be true for all numbers of a certain class (in this case, whole numbers).*

The instructional sequences in this book emphasize representation-based arguments (see Chapter 1, page 2). Such arguments are accessible to elementary-aged students and can be generalized to apply to an infinite class of numbers. For example, consider the arguments from a third-grade class for the claim, *when 1 is added to an addend and the other addend stays the same, the sum increases by 1.*

**VIDEO 3.4** The students' representations contain a fixed number of cubes. How do they convey the idea that the specific number of cubes in a stack is irrelevant? That is, what do the students say that indicates a stack can represent any number of cubes?

.................................................................

One of the students in the video, Oscar, makes an argument based on this representation. (Note that Oscar has turned this around to face the rest of the class in the video; here it's shown in its original orientation.)

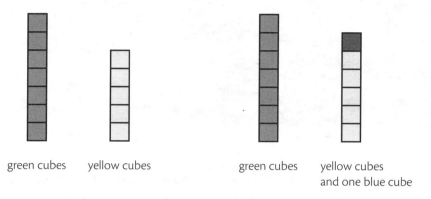

green cubes     yellow cubes         green cubes     yellow cubes
and one blue cube

Oscar explained, "This number [points to the first group of green cubes] plus this number [the first group of yellow cubes] equals the sum, then . . . the same number here [points to the second group of green cubes] plus the same number plus 1 [points to the yellow cubes plus the blue cube] equals the sum plus 1."

Oscar's argument satisfies the three characteristics of a representation-based argument, described in Chapter 1. First, the action and meaning of the operation of addition is represented as the *joining* of stacks of cubes. There are several additions: the joining of the yellow and green stacks; the joining of the single blue cube to the green stack; and the joining of the single blue cube to the yellow and green stack. Second, the argument is independent of the number of yellow or green cubes in those stacks. The representation is not just about specific quantities but can be used to show what happens with any whole numbers. Oscar makes this clear by referring to each stack as "this number" rather than naming the actual number of cubes in the stacks; that is, the yellow and green stacks can represent any two whole-number addends. Finally, the representation shows *why* the conjecture must be true. When the blue cube is added to the yellow stack (1 is added to an addend), in that same action the combined stack increases by 1 cube (the sum increases by 1).

In the elementary grades, some individual students construct general representation-based arguments like this one, but most often they result from students working together and building on each other's ideas. Mathematical argument is challenging work, and like articulating conjectures with clarity and precision, it requires the collective effort of the class. In this case, while Oscar, as an individual, appears to have a strong grasp of his argument (although notice the effort it takes for him to explain it clearly to the class), the development of his argument has benefitted from the joint work the class has done as a group as well as the time he and his partner spent constructing their representation together and explaining their argument to each other. Teachers find that students participate in discussions like this one in different ways—some students have a clear argument in mind but are working hard at stating it with precision, whereas others are strengthening their understanding of the structure of the claim and of the operation by comparing their own representations with those of other students. Through their discussions, students consider, evaluate, challenge, and justify hypotheses. They contribute different pieces of information and build upon others' explanations to jointly create a complete idea or solution.

## PHASE V: COMPARING OPERATIONS

*Once students have verified a claim, they consider the question, Does this work for other operations? Returning to Phase I, students consider a set of problems, equations, or expressions that illustrate an analogous claim for another operation. They then go on to Phases II through IV to examine and prove a conjecture about the second operation.*

We'll return to Ms. Kent's class through the last phase of the teaching model, but first, pause to conduct your own mathematical investigation. Here, instead of adding 1 to an addend, you will be considering what happens when you add 1 to a factor in a multiplication equation.

### MATHEMATICAL INVESTIGATION

| | |
|---|---|
| $7 \times 5 = 35$ <br> $7 \times 6 = 42$ | $7 \times 5 = 35$ <br> $8 \times 5 = 40$ |
| $9 \times 4 = 36$ <br> $9 \times 5 = 45$ | $9 \times 4 = 36$ <br> $10 \times 4 = 40$ |

Examine this set of related multiplication equations. What generalization about multiplication is suggested by this set of equations? Write out your statement. Using counters, a drawing, an array, or a story context, explain why this generalization must be true, no matter what multiplication expression you start with.

If students have not had experience with thinking about operations as objects that have their own properties and behaviors, they frequently think of generalizations as about *numbers* rather than about *operations*. That is, when they notice a generalization, they assume the same number patterns will occur, whether they insert the symbols, +, −, ×, or ÷. Often, after they investigate a generalization about one operation, they are surprised to discover that the same pattern does not hold for another operation. As they try to apply the same conjecture to this other operation, they run into counterexamples and realize that they must look for another regularity and state a different conjecture. Because one of the goals of this work is for students to understand more deeply the structure that is particular to each operation, it is important to explore sets of related generalizations that highlight these differences.

Depending on the grade and students' experiences with mathematical argument, investigations in which students notice, articulate, work with representations, and construct arguments for what happens when 1 (or some amount) is added to an addend might take several sessions or a few weeks. Some classes next explore what happens to the difference when 1 is added to either of the numbers of a subtraction expression (see the lesson sequence, Changing a Number in Addition or Subtraction. Ms. Kent chose to have her students explore what happens to the product when 1 is added to a factor in a multiplication expression. Her class had been begun its study of multiplication several weeks earlier, and she thought students would be able to draw on what they had been learning and deepen their understanding of multiplication through this investigation. In order to pursue the next generalization, the class went through the same four phases as before.

Ms. Kent began this second investigation in the same way she began the first. She presented her students with pairs of problems and asked what they noticed.

| | |
|---|---|
| $7 \times 5 = 35$ <br> $7 \times 6 = 42$ | $7 \times 5 = 35$ <br> $8 \times 5 = 40$ |
| $9 \times 4 = 36$ <br> $9 \times 5 = 45$ | $9 \times 4 = 36$ <br> $10 \times 4 = 40$ |

**What do you notice?**

**What's happening here?**

After some discussion, she asked students to work individually in response to this prompt: *In a multiplication problem, if you add 1 to a factor, what will happen to the product?*

Multiplication was new to the class, and not all students at first noticed the regularity evident in the problems. The following are some of the statements written by students who could see the result of adding 1 to a factor:

- The number that is not increased is the number that the answer goes up by.

- The number that is staying and not going up increases by however many it is.

- I think that the factor you increase, it goes up by the other factor.

Because some of the students were not yet able to see the regularity, Ms. Kent decided not to work on a more precise statement of the claim at this time but, instead, to investigate the equations with representations. In this way, students would develop a stronger image of multiplication and could then recognize the pattern in the arithmetic symbols. It is easy for students to write down incorrect number sentences without seeing that they are incorrect. For example, a student might write, "$7 \times 5 = 35$, so $7 \times 6 = 36$," which is not true, but the written symbols don't obviously indicate what's wrong. However, in representing these two multiplication situations, it is much more likely the student will see how $7 \times 5$ compares to $7 \times 6$, and that the product increases by more than 1.

In order to scaffold the investigation, Ms. Kent gave the following assignment.

Choose which of the original equation pairs you want to work with. Write a story for the original equation; then change it just enough to match the new equations.

Then do one of these:

- Draw a picture for the original equation, then change it just enough to match the new equations.

- Make an array for the original equation, then change it just enough to match the new equations.

**Example:** Original equation $7 \times 5 = 35$
New equations $7 \times 6 = 42, 8 \times 5 = 40$

Students worked in pairs and then came together to share their work, each pair presenting their story problem and picture or array. Eduardo and Sam's story was, "There are 7 groups of 5 fish living in the store. There are 35 fish living in the store." For this, they drew a diagram that showed 7 groups of 5.

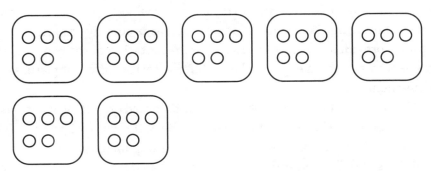

To change the story to $8 \times 5$, they said that 1 more group of fish came, increasing the total by 5. They showed the new group of fish by coloring it.

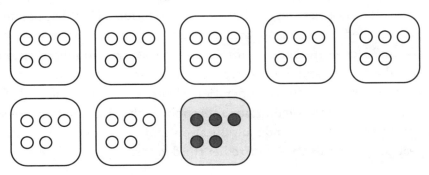

Then, to change $7 \times 5$ to $7 \times 6$, the boys said that 1 more fish was added to each group of fish. They indicated the additional fish in their picture by showing a black dot in each group. When 5 increased to 6, there were 7 additional fish in the store.

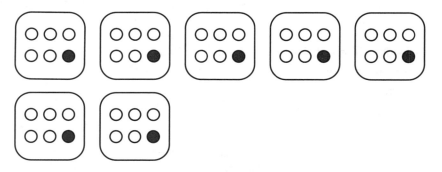

Before continuing to read, think about Eduardo and Sam's story context for yourself. Their story and representation show what happens when 1 is added to a factor, using the specific equation, $7 \times 5 = 35$. Does their representation have the potential to be part of a representation-based argument for any whole numbers?

## MATHEMATICAL INVESTIGATION

How could Eduardo and Sam's story problems and diagrams be extended to illustrate the generalizations you stated in the mathematical investigation on page 39?

Many of the students had story contexts and diagrams like Eduardo and Sam's. Some of the students presented arrays to show what happens when you add one row or one column. This is a context in which it was productive to linger. Each pair's presentation provided the class with a new representation of the concept, solidifying the ideas as they saw them expressed in different stories, different pictures, and different arrangements of cubes.

Throughout the presentations, the class worked on stating what was taking place: When 1 is added to 7, the product increases by 5, the size of 1 group. When 1 is added to 5, the product increases by 7 because each group increases by 1. By the end of their discussions of different representations, they had developed a more general class conjecture: *When the first factor increases by 1, the product increases by 1 group equal to the second factor. When the second factor increases by 1, each group is 1 larger, so the product increases by the number of groups, the first factor.*

Now the class had engaged in two investigations: (1) What happens to the sum when 1 is added to an addend? and (2) what happens to the product when 1 is added to a factor? However, students may remember these two investigations as distinct, unrelated activities and not necessarily reflect back on what they have learned about the difference between the two operations. For that reason, at the end of the sequence, after students present their arguments about multiplication, they are asked to think back about their addition and multiplication conjectures and arguments. In this video, the teacher poses this challenge to her third graders.

**| FOCUS QUESTION**

**VIDEO 3.5** How would you answer the teacher's question about the difference between adding some amount to an addend and adding some amount to a factor?

Video 3.5 ▶

http://hein.pub/WDIW3.5

..............................................................

The teacher's question prompted students to articulate how multiplication differs from addition. When adding two numbers, the addends refer to the same unit: $7 + 5 = 12$ might mean 7 fish joined with 5 fish to make a group of 12 fish. However, when multiplying two numbers, the factors refer to different units: $7 \times 5$ might mean 7 *groups* each containing 5 *fish*, to make 35 fish altogether.

Ms. Kent's class used the lesson sequence, Changing a Number in Addition or Multiplication, to work through the five phases of the teaching model for mathematical argument. These Algebra and Proof lessons, as they were called in her classroom, were spaced over the fall semester in about twenty-five 20-minute sessions.

## WHAT STUDENTS GAIN

As students move through the five phases of mathematical argument, they develop the mathematical habit of noticing patterns and regularities. They engage in articulating their ideas and claims with precision as they write class conjectures. They learn to investigate the structure underlying the patterns they notice by examining examples, and they create representations to move from examining examples with specific numbers to making general arguments.

At the same time, students think deeply about the operations as mathematical objects, each with its own set of properties and behaviors. As students articulate their conjectures, they gradually realize that it is important to specify the operation(s) involved. Later, in Phases III and IV, students' representations embody the action and relationships of the operation. When they compare addition and multiplication in Phase V, it becomes clearer to students that the patterns they notice apply to particular operations.

Through these explorations, students develop a stronger sense of how the number system works with different operations. When students solve calculation problems, they are then better able to determine what a reasonable answer would be and can correct strategies that do not work. Later, when students begin algebra, they will be prepared to recognize the same behaviors of the operations as they learn to work with algebraic symbols.

The next chapter presents the five phases of the teaching model but now from the perspective of a teacher using the sequence, Same Sum, Same Difference. Based on the writing of collaborating teachers, it conveys the teacher's perceptions, decisions, and reflections as she engages her students in investigations of addition and subtraction.

## CHAPTER FOCUS QUESTIONS

*Use these questions to think back over Chapter 3 as a whole, including the classroom examples and video clips.*

1. Consider the five phases of the teaching model for mathematical argument discussed in this chapter. How does each phase focus on a different aspect of the mathematics? What does each phase contribute to students' deepening understanding of mathematical argument and the operations?

2. What did you notice about your own process investigating the mathematics for yourself? What did you get from comparing your representations to those of the students in the chapter (or, if you are reading this book with a group, to those of other adults)?

# 4

# Using the Lesson Sequences: What the Teacher Does

Just as the goals of noticing, articulating, representing, and proving a generalization bring students into new ways of engaging with mathematics, so, too, do they bring new challenges for teachers. How do teachers invite students into this process? How do they draw students' attention to critical features of a generalization, articulation, or representation? On what basis do they make decisions about how to focus whole-group discussion? What aspects of individual students' thinking are important to track? In Chapter 4, we again work through the five phases of the teaching model, this time with an eye toward where the teacher's attention is focused, decisions she makes, and actions she takes.

The examples in this chapter are a composite drawn from first-person narratives written by collaborating teachers. These narratives, based on recordings and notes taken during the lessons, convey the students' and teacher's words and actions, as well as the teacher's in-the-moment reasoning and reflections. For the purposes of this chapter, the narratives of third-grade teachers who taught the sequence, Same Sum, Same Difference, are combined to create a single voice belonging to a character we have named Lauren Fried. We have chosen to present this chapter as a first-person narrative to convey the teachers' perceptions, decisions, and reflections. In each phase, we follow the example with our commentary on the teacher's moves and the importance of the decisions she made.

In addition to the narrative, we provide links to videos from classrooms engaged in the same lessons. You might pause your reading to view and reflect on the clips, or you might prefer to read through the chapter first and then return to consider the video examples.

Before you continue reading, take time to investigate the mathematics content of the first part of the sequence, Same Sum, Same Difference, used to illustrate this chapter.

## MATHEMATICAL INVESTIGATION

Examine this set of addition equations.

| | |
|---|---|
| $9 + 4 = 13$ <br> $8 + 5 = 13$ | $9 + 4 = 13$ <br> $10 + 3 = 13$ |
| $23 + 19 = 42$ <br> $22 + 20 = 42$ | $23 + 19 = 42$ <br> $24 + 18 = 42$ |

What generalization about equivalent addition expressions does these pairs of equations suggest?

Write out your statement. Using counters, a drawing, a number line, or a story context, explain why this generalization must be true, no matter what addition expression you start with.

# PHASE I: NOTICING REGULARITY

*Students examine pairs or sequences of related problems, equations, or expressions and describe patterns they notice.*

As described earlier, the work begins with cultivating in students the habit of looking for and expressing regularity. An investigation begins with the teacher asking the class to examine sets of equations, expressions, or problems that embody the relationship to be explored. The teacher draws out ideas about what students notice and brings students' attention to the relationships under study. By the end of this phase, students have enough of an idea of the structure shared by the examples they have considered that they are ready to articulate a conjecture. As you read, particularly look for how the teacher:

- listens to and validates students' initial ideas

- focuses students' attention on relationships among the equations, expressions, or problems

- poses questions to move students toward the generalization to be studied.

We begin the story of Lauren Fried's work with her students as she initiates the sequence.

Throughout this and the later phases, notice the extent to which the teacher attends to students' thinking. In the language of one of our collaborators, teachers must *hear*, rather than "under-hear" (missing the content of what the student is trying to communicate or assuming the student doesn't understand because the wording is unclear) or "over-hear" (assuming more content or a deeper understanding than what the student intended). The examples convey what the teachers saw and heard from students and what the teachers did in response.

### Ms. Fried's Class: Noticing Regularity

I have just begun a new sequence, Same Sum, Same Difference, which begins with a focus on a generalization involving equivalent addition expressions: *Given an addition expression, when one addend increases by some amount and the other addend decreases by the same amount, the sum remains the same.* Many of my students have been using this idea in their calculations. For example, when solving $198 + 433$, students might say, "I took 2 from 433 and gave it to the 198 to make $200 + 431$, and that's easy to add. It's 631." Although this strategy has been presented in class, we have never examined it as a generalization that applies to any addition expression. Students who use this strategy regularly may not have thought about *why* this relationship holds, or that it applies only to the operation of addition and not subtraction, multiplication, or division. Studying this generalization will give all students access to the reasoning that underlies the calculation strategy and will engage all students in the practice of noticing regularity, articulating a conjecture with precision, and constructing a viable argument to prove the conjecture.

I told the class we would be engaged with a new kind of activity that we would call Algebra and Proof sessions. "Algebra," I said, "involves noticing ways the operations work. We would talk about things we noticed and then work to prove that they were true. Each time we return to the lesson sequence (Mondays, Wednesdays, and Fridays, directly after lunch), I'll let the class know we are doing an Algebra and Proof session and remind them of where we were at the end of the last session."

I began the investigation by posting the following expressions and question:

$$1 + 14$$
$$2 + 13$$
$$3 + 12$$
$$4 + 11$$

### What do you notice about these expressions?

I paused for several seconds to make sure everyone had time to think and then called on James, who said, "There's a 4 in the first one and the last one, and there's a 3 is the second and third. But they're in different places."

Whenever I've begun an investigation of a generalization, students would specify where particular digits appear in a pattern without considering how they are related to each other. Thus, I didn't expect the first observations to approach the underlying structure in the list of expressions. Rather, during these first minutes I welcomed all observations so that students would get a chance to become familiar with the expressions in the list, and I would get to hear what students first noticed. In order to validate James' observation, I asked him to come to the board to point to what he saw. Then I was ready to hear from another student.

Roberta said, "You can switch the numbers around. Like 1 + 14 can be switched to 14 + 1." This observation was relevant to the commutative property of addition, a concept worthy of investigation another time, but not today. I asked Roberta, too, to come to the board to point out what she meant and then heard from the next student.

When Melody said, "The first numbers are going 1, 2, 3, 4," I asked her to point to her pattern, too. Although Melody referred only to the first addend, her comment addressed how the expressions change from one to the next, providing an opening for me. I said, "Melody pointed out that the first addend goes 1, 2, 3, 4. If we follow this pattern, what will the next expression be?" Continuing the pattern required students to look at the whole expression and the patterns in the sequence. Students identified the next two expressions.

$$1 + 14$$
$$2 + 13$$
$$3 + 12$$
$$4 + 11$$
$$5 + 10$$
$$6 + 9$$

Adam said, "One number goes up and the other goes down."

I asked, "And what about the sums?"

Several students called out that they all equal 15.

At this point, we had the aspects of this list of expressions relevant to the generalization we were to explore: As one addend increases by 1 and the other addend decreases by 1, the total remains the same. However, the students had simply noticed a pattern among this particular set of numbers and might not have extended their thinking to other sequences with the same characteristics. The work to come would be to see this same pattern in addition expressions with other numbers and in a variety of representations.

My next move was to provide an image of these particular expressions that showed the changing quantities and how they are related. I presented a stack of 15 cubes and asked the class to look carefully as I removed 1 cube from the stack to create a stack of 14 and a stack of 1. I asked, "Do you see an expression that matches these cubes? How could you change these cubes to show the next expression?" Students suggested moving 1 cube from the stack of 14 to make a representation of 2 + 13.

I wanted the students to look at the change in the numerical expressions *together with* the change in the cube stacks to see how they match. It is through this correspondence, looking at the

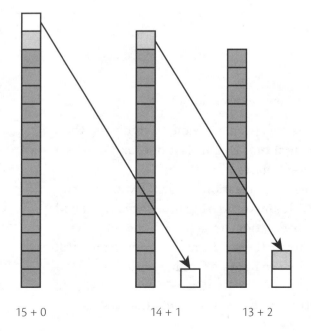

15 + 0                    14 + 1              13 + 2

cubes and the symbols together, that students infuse the symbols with meaning and will be able to see *why* the patterns in the symbols hold. Later in the sequence, it is with such representations that students will construct arguments for why the generalization is true. For now, I wanted my students to notice how the quantities in the expressions were changing and how those changing quantities looked when represented with cubes. Several students were commenting on how the cubes matched the expressions when Elsa called out, "Oh, I have an idea! You could do it with other numbers."

I suspected Elsa was able to see that it didn't matter how many cubes there were, that each time 1 cube was moved, one stack decreased by 1 and the other increased by 1. But from other students' body language and facial expressions, my sense was that the rest of the class wasn't ready to move so quickly. I asked Elsa to write down her idea on her scratch pad so that she wouldn't forget it.

Soon, a few other students were saying, "Oh!" I wasn't sure what they had noticed, but it was too close to the end of the session to discuss more ideas. Rather than continue as a whole class, I said, "I see that several of you have more thoughts about what's going on here. If you have an idea, I want you to write it down." I'd be able to look at their scratch pads later to see their ideas.

I concluded the lesson by saying, "I have something I want all of you to do. I want you to work individually to create addition expressions equal to 24 with two addends. I'd like you to start with 1 + 23 and see what happens." But time was up. In our next session, I will give students time to create two-addend addition expressions equal to 24. As they work individually, I will be able to see where individual students are. Are they able to recognize the same pattern in another set of expressions? Can they create other sequences that exhibit the same regularity? Are they moving toward a conjecture about what happens to the sum when one addend is increased by 1 and the other is decreased by 1?

### Commentary: Noticing Regularity

As illustrated by Ms. Fried's account, the noticing phase begins with students making observations about a sequence of addition expressions. Each student who volunteered an observation was asked to come to the board to point to the numbers he or she was referring to, thus validating the student's thinking while not derailing the conversation. This move allowed Ms. Fried to make sure she understood what the student said, not assuming too much or too little. Furthermore, she maintained focus on each student's idea long enough so that classmates could follow. As students' comments moved in the direction of the generalization to be investigated, the teacher posed questions to draw students' attention to how the expressions change in relation to each other: "If we follow the pattern, what will the next expression be?" "What happens to the sum?"

Representing the expressions with stacks of cubes allowed students to construct deeper meaning for the numerical expressions. *Seeing* the quantities (as opposed to reading numerals) and following what happens to the stacks as the two addends change reveal the relationships in a way that symbols on the page do not. Two stacks of cubes will always have the same total when a cube from one stack is moved to the other. The work of the students at this stage is to see how the cube stacks reflect the symbols on the board—how moving a single cube from one stack to another matches subtracting

1 from one addend and adding 1 to the other. As they make these connections, some students begin to picture the same pattern with other numbers.

Ms. Fried ended the first lesson by giving the class a new task: to work individually to list a new set of addition expressions to see if the same pattern holds. This task provided all students an opportunity to extend their thinking from wherever they currently were. Some students would focus on the new set of specific numbers, while others would begin to formulate a generalization. By interacting with students as they worked on their own, the teacher would be able to assess where individuals were in their thinking and get a sense of the class as a whole.

...........................................................................

The following video clips show classes working at the noticing phase of the Same Sum, Same Difference sequence. You might watch the clips multiple times. First, listen to understand what the students are saying. Then watch the clips to think about the teacher's moves.

The first two clips come from the first day of the sequence.

## FOCUS QUESTIONS

**VIDEO 4.1** Abigail, Sanger, Sarah, Ben, and Alex have offered ideas. What are they? How is each contribution different, and how are they related? In what ways does the teacher encourage students to voice their ideas? What ideas does she highlight in her comments?

http://hein.pub/WDIW4.1

The teacher asks the class to continue the list. 5 + 8 and 6 + 7 are added. Then the teacher introduces a representation with cubes.

## FOCUS QUESTIONS

**VIDEO 4.2** What does the cube representation offer the students? What new insights might they derive from seeing the numbers and operations represented in this way? What does the teacher do to draw in students? How do her questions and comments highlight ideas that will move students toward a conjecture?

http://hein.pub/WDIW4.2

The next clip comes from the second day of the sequence in a different classroom. Students examine addition expressions equal to 24 alongside addition expressions equal to 15.

## FOCUS QUESTIONS

**VIDEO 4.3** How does the teacher encourage an open discussion of what the students are noticing? How does she draw attention to the relationships that will become the focus of the investigation? In what ways does she foster students making connections between each other's ideas?

http://hein.pub/WDIW4.3

...........................................................................

## PHASE II: ARTICULATING A CLAIM

*Based on the patterns noticed in Phase I, students work individually and collectively to write a conjecture clear enough so that someone not in the class could understand it.*

Once students have had an opportunity to notice a pattern related to the behavior of an operation, they work to write a clear statement about what that pattern is—a statement that would be comprehensible to someone outside the class who had not participated in the discussions. This statement is a conjecture, a claim they believe is true for a class of numbers but has yet to be proved.

As you read the following account of the articulating phase, particularly look for how Ms. Fried:

- provides support for students to make initial formulations

- selects a few formulations to be critiqued and edited to create a class conjecture

- offers challenges or suggestions to help students revise the statements to produce a conjecture at an appropriate level of precision.

### Ms. Fried's Class: Articulating a Claim

My students have explored two-addend expressions equal to 15 and 24 and discussed the patterns they noticed. Then, I asked them to work individually to write a statement about the pattern. This is the first time they have been asked to come up with language to express a generalization. It is challenging work.

When I reviewed my students' writing, I found that most of their statements were vague: "The numbers change." "They all have the same answer." "Some numbers go up and some numbers go down." One statement, "8 becomes 9 and 7 becomes 6, and then it's 15" included both what changed and what stayed constant but addressed only specific numbers, referring to 8 + 7 and 9 + 6.

I appreciated my students' efforts, and I can see ideas behind their words, but I didn't find enough to provide a starting point from which the class could work to formulate a conjecture. For this reason, I departed from the planned lesson sequence and gave time for students to collaborate and further develop their thoughts. I set up students in small groups and provided another set of equations to consider, suggesting they discuss what is happening in the equations before recording their thinking. I presented the examples in the format of equations, hoping this would prompt students to focus more on equivalence rather than just the change in addends.

$$9 + 11 = 10 + 10$$

$$14 + 16 = 15 + 15$$

$$19 + 19 = 20 + 18$$

$$20 + 30 = 21 + 29$$

$$21 + 29 = 22 + 28$$

After sharing their observations with peers, students' statements were richer, and I selected a few to bring to the next session.

- If you take away a number and add one number, it will equal the same answer.

- If you have two numbers and have a sum and want to have the same sum with a smaller number, then you have to bring the first addend down and bring the second addend up.

- If you take away 1 from a number and add 1 to a number, it should equal the same answer.

These general statements contained descriptions of both what changes and what stays the same—elements necessary to create a conjecture. They also had limitations, which would be important to bring to the class' attention. We were now ready to work together to create a class conjecture.

I posted the three statements on the board and had students read each one aloud. After some initial discussion, the class chose to focus on the third statement.

My first concern was that the statement didn't specify the operation. In students' work on calculation, they often focus on numbers, and the operations fall to the background. I needed to draw their attention to the importance of the operation in the generalization they were working on. I wrote *9* and *16* on the board, with no operation sign. I read the first part of the statement, *if you take away 1 from a number*, and said, "So let's say I have the number 9 and I take one away so it's 8." And I read the next part of the statement, *and add 1 to a number,* and said, "Let's say I have the number 16 and I add one so it's 17. It says it should equal the same answer. Is this the rule we're talking about?"

9̶ 8

1̶6̶ 17

Several students shook their heads no, while others nodded their heads yes. I wasn't sure if they were trying to read my affect or were thinking through the ideas for themselves. I said, "It seems to me there's something missing here."

Melody said, "So when you minus that 1 and add it to the 17, you're not wasting any ones. You're not taking away anything."

Melody had a clear image that the total quantity was conserved, but nobody remarked on the missing addition sign. I said, "Okay, but where does it say we're adding these numbers together?" When Jacob acknowledged it didn't say that, I invited the class to edit. "What should we add to this sentence?"

Once they realized they needed to specify the operation, students offered a few ideas and edited the statement so that it now read, *If you have two addends and you take away 1 from one and add 1 to one, it should equal the same sum.*

But there are other interpretations of those words than what the class intended. I asked, "So does this mean if I take 1 away from 9 and get 8, like I did before, and then add 1 back to the 8 again, the sum will be the same?"

Although it's true that I get back the same expression, 9 + 16, and it still equals 25, that's not what the class had intended. In response to my challenge, they revised their statement again: *If you have two addends, and you take away 1 from one and add 1 to the other one it should equal the same sum.*

The class was now satisfied that this statement communicated their idea, but I wanted to push them still further, to clarify the referents. I said, "That sounds like a lot of 'ones.' What are we really talking about when we say, 'away from one and add it to the other one'?"

After more discussion, the class revised again: *If you have two addends, and you take away 1 from an addend and add 1 to the other addend it should equal the same sum.*

Ezra pointed out that *addend* was repeated too often and it didn't sound good. In our language arts lessons, we had been talking about not using the same word repeatedly in creative writing. I assume Ezra was thinking about those discussions. Dede offered to check the thesaurus. Nancy said they should try using the word *number* instead, but the class rejected the idea when they tried it, saying that now, "It doesn't say we're adding." At this point, we all agreed to keep this statement as our class conjecture.

To wrap up, the class read over the conjecture again and checked it with other expressions.

## Commentary: Articulating a Claim

In this lesson, Ms. Fried encouraged students to write their initial ideas about patterns they noticed in the expressions they had examined. When their statements were too vague and incomplete to use as starting points for devising a class conjecture, she realized her students needed more time on this phase. It was the first time they had been asked to come up with language to describe a generalization, and Ms. Fried gave them an extra session to work together to test out ideas. She set up her students in small groups with another set of equations to discuss, and with that support, they wrote statements that were more developed.

Ms. Fried didn't expect this additional time to result in a statement clear enough to stand as a class conjecture without further discussion. In fact, even if there had been a clear and precise statement, a teacher might choose to have the class work from one that was not complete—for it is in the act of critiquing and revising that students learn how to select language to communicate their idea. In this lesson, we see how Ms. Fried challenged the students with questions and interpretations that prompted them to produce a more precisely worded conjecture. In the future, as students gain experience, they learn what to look for to produce a clear conjecture. In particular, students come to see that as they describe the relationships among quantities, they must specify the operation(s) under consideration and be clear about referents. When they work on the second conjecture of the sequence, they are likely to be able to initiate more of the suggestions themselves.

The goal in this process is not to formulate the most concise or precise statement possible. After all, the teacher could present a conjecture to the students, and they might even understand it. Rather, the goal is to have students learn to communicate, which means they must take on the task of putting *their* ideas into words. Especially if students have never before been asked to articulate a generalization, they need time, encouragement, and opportunities to try out their ideas without judgment or pressure to use specific language. After the students have initial statements to work with, the teacher challenges them to edit their claims at an appropriate level of precision with language that this particular class can use at this particular time. She takes the opportunity to introduce or review mathematical terms that students might find useful in their statements. She especially draws students' attention to referents, such as "one" and "other one," that need greater clarity.

It is important to keep in mind that technical language supports communication when students can use it fluently. In order to develop fluency, students must have opportunities to use it frequently. If the vocabulary is unfamiliar, it might get in the way. Some of our teacher collaborators reported that when the class conjecture used new vocabulary, they posted it together with a version that used less formal terms. That way, all students had access to the idea and, at the same time, had exposure to new terminology. For example, in another class using the Same Sum, Same Difference sequence, the students produced the following conjecture: "When we have an expression, we can change the numbers but still have the same answer. The numbers can go up and down. We change the numbers by making one less and the other one bigger. We can take away 1 and then add 1. We could switch a 3. 30 + 53 = 33 + 50." As seen in the next photo, edits (in smaller handwriting) specify that the expression is an *addition* expression, that the answer is a *sum*, and that 1 is taken away from *one of the addends* and 1 is added *to the other addend*.

When we have an <sub>addition</sub> expression, we can change the numbers but still have the same answer. The numbers can go up and down. We change the numbers by making one less and the other bigger. We can take away one <sub>from one of the addends</sub> and then add one. <sub>to the other addend</sub>

We could switch a 3. 30+53= 33+50

## PHASE III: INVESTIGATING THROUGH REPRESENTATIONS

*Students represent specific instances of the claim with manipulatives, diagrams, or story contexts.*

To solidify their understanding of the generalization, in this phase students create representations—in the form of objects, drawings, diagrams, number lines, arrays, and/or story contexts—that embody the relationships described in the conjecture. Such representations become tools for thinking and communication and will be the basis of general arguments they will produce in the following phase.

In the example of lessons during the representing phase, look for how Ms. Fried:

- supports students as they make first attempts to represent the class conjecture

- uses small-group time to assess what students understand and intervenes (poses questions or offers suggestions) to extend their ideas

- recognizes which representations or story contexts are especially useful to illustrate the ideas of the conjecture and selects a range of representations to discuss with the class

- asks questions in the whole group that help students recognize where the components of the conjecture and the numerical expressions appear in the representations.

### Ms. Fried's Class: Investigating Through Representations

Now that the class had formulated a conjecture, the next phase of the work was to represent particular instances of the generalization. I asked for volunteers to briefly remind the class about the idea we were working on; then I had a student read our conjecture aloud. I assigned pairs and asked them to represent the equation $23 + 9 = 22 + 10$ using a picture, cubes, a number line, or a story context. As I went from group to group, I took note of the representations students had created and listened to them talk about their ideas. I decided how or whether to intervene, based on how they explained their representation.

Jackson and Maria created two story problems.

*On Saturday, we go to the park and see 23 children on the swings and 9 children on the climbing structure. We see 32 children.*

*On Sunday, we go to the park and see 22 children on the swings and 10 children on the climbing structure. We see 32 children.*

Although the two problems fit the two equations—$23 + 9 = 32$ and $22 + 10 = 32$—they do not illustrate how $23 + 9$ can be transformed into $22 + 10$. That is, the representation does not provide insight into *why* the total stays the same when one addend decreases by 1 and the other increases by 1. After listening to Jackson and Maria explain how their stories matched the equations, I wanted to ask them something that would move them toward the explanation of *why*. "If you know that $23 + 9 = 32$, is there a way to know what $22 + 10$ must be, without adding the numbers? Let's say we're still at Saturday and you see 23 children on the swings and 9 children on the climbing structure. Can those same kids move around to show $22 + 10$?" I didn't know if my questions would help Jackson and Maria think about how the two situations are related, or if they would continue to see each expression as distinct situations. In the moment, I promised myself I'd circle back around to them.

Latesha and Sage also created a story context.

*Sage has 23 candies in her bag and Latesha has 9 candies in a cup. Sage wants to share her candy with Latesha so she asks her mom for permission.*

The girls had piles of counters representing Sage's candies in her bag and Latesha's candies in her cup and moved one counter to demonstrate the transformation of 23 + 9 into 22 + 10. They realized they could keep going, repeatedly transferring one counter from the bag to the cup. With each transfer, they announced that they still had the same number of candies because they hadn't eaten any yet.

In this context, all the components of the conjecture—that one addend decreases by 1, that one addend increases by 1, and that the total remains constant—are present in the single act of moving one candy from the bag to the cup. In that movement, one can see that the sum *necessarily* remains fixed. That is, for these specific numbers, it demonstrates why the conjecture is true.

The eventual goal is to have students recognize how the numerical expressions and the components of the conjecture appear in the representation, for it is in those connections that the argument lies. However, sometimes when students create contexts, the contexts become a separate world, disconnected from the symbols and the conjecture. At this point, I wasn't sure whether the girls were making those connections. In order to encourage them to move in that direction, I asked Sage and Latesha to specify the arithmetic in each stage of their story. "You started with the problem 23 + 9. What are the other addition expressions you acted out in your story?" Making those connections would be an important part of the whole-group discussion we would have about the representations.

Roberta and James were working with two stacks of cubes. When I sat down with them, Roberta started talking about some of the ideas that had come up in the earlier class discussion that led to the conjecture. She started out saying, "You know, you could change the 1 either way." When I asked her to explain what she meant, she blurted out a whole string of thoughts: "I think that if we looked at 23 + 9, I could move 1 from the 23 and give it to the 9 to make 22 + 10. But I could also move 1 from the 9 and move it to the 23 to make 24 + 8. You could also take 2 away and move that around. Actually, you could take any amount away and move it. I think you just want to make a friendly number. It works all of the time."

Now that she was using cubes to represent and think about the patterns in the symbols, Roberta was having several new insights. In an earlier class discussion, Roberta had specified that if 1 is taken from the *greater* addend and added to the *lesser* addend, the total stays the same. Now that she was looking at a representation that showed how the quantities changed, she realized it didn't matter which addend increased or decreased. Second, with the stacks of cubes in front of her, she realized you could move 2, or *any amount*, from one addend to the other. And then she recognized this phenomenon as the calculation strategy she already used when she'd change addends to make "friendly" numbers that are easier to work with.

With this barrage of ideas, I was concerned about what James was thinking. When I asked him, he shrugged and said he didn't follow what Roberta had said. James was holding two stacks of cubes, 22 and 10, and I asked him what they meant. He said, "Put them together and you have 22 + 10. I can move one cube back and get 23 + 9."

I asked James to explain to Roberta how the sequence would continue and to write down the next addition expressions. This would help James connect the representation with symbols, and it would help Roberta slow down to let her new insights sink in.

At the same time that I was listening to pairs, I was planning the whole-group discussion, deciding which representations to share with the class and what questions to ask. I chose to begin with Sage and Latesha's story context for several reasons. First, this was among those representations that demonstrate *why* the change of addends results in a constant sum. A variation of their story could eventually be used as the basis of a proof, which will come up in the next phase of the teaching model. Second, the story has a clear referent for each of the addends and the sum—the number of Latesha's or Sage's candies and the number of candies between them—supporting clear communication in the class discussion. Third, Latesha and Sage had been quiet in the last few class discussions, and I wanted to put their work in the forefront.

After Sage and Latesha presented the story, I brought the class back to the conjecture and asked a series of core questions to make explicit the correspondences between components of the conjecture and components of the representation.

- Where in the story do you see the two addends of the conjecture?

- How does the representation show that 9 was added to 23?

- Where do you see the sum?

- Where do you see one addend increasing by 1?

- Where do you see the other addend decreasing by 1?

- How do you know the sum stays the same?

After discussion of the story, I selected one of the cube-stack representations and posed the same questions. And then I asked the class to compare the two representations: "Can Latesha's and Sage's candies be seen in Max's cube stacks? Where do you see in the cubes that the number of candies stays the same?"

After looking at several representations of $23 + 9 = 22 + 10$, I asked the class to consider another pair of addition expressions. "What would change in the representation in order to show $13 + 8 = 12 + 9$?" I wanted my students to recognize the structure of the representations—those aspects that stay the same even as the numbers change.

By the end of the discussion, I was curious about whether the class would be ready to work with representations that could prove the general claim, which we will be exploring in the next phase.

### Commentary: *Investigating Through Representations*

In this example, we see that as students worked on representations of the class conjecture, Ms. Fried had two goals in mind: (1) that students illustrate how one expression is transformed into the other (e.g., how $23 + 9$ is transformed into $22 + 10$) to demonstrate the necessity of the conclusion (that the sum remains the same), and (2) that students see correspondences across the numerical expressions, components of the conjecture, and components of the representation. As she moved from group to group, she assessed where students stood with respect to those goals and posed questions or offered suggestions to move their thinking forward. At the same time, she noted representations and listened to students' ideas to structure the class discussion.

When leading the whole-group discussion, Ms. Fried posed questions with the same goals in mind. For each representation that was shared, she presented a set of core questions, asking students to specify how the representation connected to the equivalent expressions and to the components of the conjecture. Even though she asked these same questions each time, it did not feel like repetition to the students. Each time they were concentrating on making sense of a different representation as well as considering what different representations had in common. By thinking through the same set of questions, they were internalizing a framework that would help them learn what it means to represent a conjecture.

Once students understood several representations with one set of numbers, Ms. Fried asked them to consider the same representations with another set of numbers. By drawing or imagining how the representations work with different quantities, students began to notice the structure of the representations—how they work for numbers of any size. The next step brings them to proof—how to use a representation to demonstrate why the conjecture must be true for any numbers.

..................................................................

In the video below, we see the whole-group discussion of another classroom at the representation phase of the teaching model. As you watch the following clips, consider this question: How does the teacher engage a wide variety of students and, at the same time, maintain focus on a progression of ideas?

## ▎FOCUS QUESTIONS

Video 4.4 ▶

http://hein.pub/WDIW4.4

**VIDEO 4.4, SECTION 1**   How do the two story contexts represent the relationship between 20 + 4 and 19 + 5? What do the visual images along with the story contexts offer? What is important about the teacher's questions?

**VIDEO 4.4, SECTION 2**   In this clip, Brage, Naomi, and Justin make comments.

What point does each student make? Why is it useful for the teacher to ask students to comment on their classmates' observations?

**VIDEO 4.4, SECTION 3**   What does Elena's demonstration offer the class? Why might the teacher have chosen to write down Elena's words?

**VIDEO 4.4, SECTION 4**   What is the point that Leo, Nevea, and Reid are making, and why is it an important point to make? How has the teacher used what she heard in small groups to enrich the whole-group discussion?

**VIDEO 4.4, SECTION 5**   What is important about Selena's mention of proof? Why does the teacher ask the class to discuss this in pairs?

..................................................................

## PHASE IV: CONSTRUCTING ARGUMENTS

*Students use their representations to explain why the conjecture must be true for all numbers of a certain class (in this case, whole numbers).*

In Ms. Fried's class, during the representing phase of the teaching model, while the class worked in pairs to create representations, one student, Isaac, held up stacks of 23 and 9 cubes, moved 1 cube from one stack to the other, and pointed out that the total stayed the same. When the teacher asked if that model could be used to show another example, Isaac said, "I don't even think we have to change the numbers of the cubes. I think we could just pretend they were our new numbers." This idea—that a stack of cubes, or a blob drawn on a page, or a bag holding candies, could represent *any* number—is key to using representations as proof of a generalization.

The notion of proof is new to most elementary students, and some may not understand the purpose of it. The goal at this phase of the learning model is to deepen students' understanding of the conjecture, to have them consider what it means to make a claim for an infinite class of numbers, and to engage them in discussion of representations that could be used to prove their conjecture.

In the continuing example, look for how the teacher:

- communicates the goal of proving in a way that brings students into the activity

- selects representations to share that have the potential to prove the conjecture

- keeps track of students' ideas regarding what it means to prove a conjecture for an infinite class of numbers.

### Ms. Fried's Class: Constructing Arguments

In our Algebra and Proof sessions up until now, we've been exploring a generalization using small numbers familiar to my students. I have wanted their focus to be on relationships between expressions, not distracted by managing numbers larger than they could easily picture. But now, in order to move them into the idea of proof, I wanted them to think about what it means to make a conjecture that applies to all numbers (in this case, all whole numbers), no matter how large. So I asked the class to think about these questions, which I had posted:

- What numbers does our conjecture work for?

- Does our conjecture work for really big numbers?

- How do you know?

- What is the largest number you think our conjecture will work with?

This was at the end of a long day in which students were working hard, but they were willing to take on my questions, and I learned a few things. First, those who spoke claimed that the conjecture will work for all numbers, as long as we stay in the realm of positive numbers. (They pointed out that if one of the addends is 0, for example, we can't subtract from 0—at least not without moving into a realm these students don't yet understand.) Second, when I asked about the "biggest number," several students explained that there's no such thing as a biggest number. I'm not sure how many students have considered that question, but the idea of infinity was in the air. Third, two students began to construct general arguments about taking some away and then giving the same amount back.

I had an inkling of the ideas of only those students who spoke, less than half the class. But I had given them all questions to begin thinking about. I left the questions posted so that they could reread them and continue mulling them over.

In the next session, I reminded students about our discussion and drew their attention again to the posted questions. I asked students to work in pairs to use a representation—either a version of those they created in previous sessions or new ones—to make the case that the conjecture is true for all whole numbers, no matter how large. I suggested they think about convincing someone who has not been in our discussions—our principal, for example—that our conjecture must be true.

Most students dug into the task, and by the end of the lesson, several pairs had come up with strong arguments. However, not everyone understood what the task was about. James and Natalie, in particular, felt completely frustrated, not knowing what they were being asked to do. "You can't show it for *all* numbers," James proclaimed. "It's impossible."

I felt that it was important that everyone in the class enter the whole-group discussion with an idea of what a representation-based argument can be. For this reason, for the next session I decided to combine partner pairs into groups of six to discuss their arguments. All students would see a variety of ideas, and those who had been floundering would get a foothold. I put James and Natalie in a group that included Melody and Karen because of the clarity of their cube representation and their ability to explain it. I checked in on that group several times during the lesson and saw James and Natalie engaged in the discussion. Their affect was completely different from the day before.

I began the next lesson by reminding the class of the work they had been doing in small groups: to create a proof that our conjecture always works. Today we would be sharing the proofs. "For each proof, we should be able to see how the representation shows addition, how it shows the two addends being combined, how it shows that if one addend is increasing by 1 the other addend is decreasing by 1, and how it shows that you get the same sum. So our work together today is to see if we understand other people's representations and decide if we accept them as proof." I wanted to emphasize these two essential questions: (1) How does the representation incorporate the components of the conjecture? and (2) is the argument convincing?

I decided to begin with Melody and Karen's proof for several reasons. They used a cube model with which, by now, all students had experience, and I was confident they could relate it to the components of the conjecture. The clarity of the model would allow the class to focus on the new aspect of their representations: that a stack of cubes could represent *any number*. I also wanted to start the conversation with a representation James and Natalie had already explored.

Melody presented a long stick of red cubes and a long stick of blue cubes as her two addends. She said, "Our model shows that we don't know how many cubes are on the stick. We don't actually! And if we take this many," removing some red cubes, "and put it onto there," adding them to the blue stick, "it would be the same thing. The red one got smaller and the blue one got bigger, and it's the same."

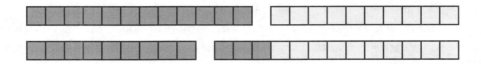

I thought the class could see that the representation showed one addend decreasing by a fixed amount and the other increasing by that same amount, but I didn't know if the conclusion—that the total stayed the same—was getting lost. I repeated Melody's words, "The red one got smaller and the blue one got bigger, and it's the same. What does Melody mean by *it*? What is the same?"

Jackson said, "It's all the same cubes. All the cubes stayed, and nothing else came in."

I asked the class, "How convincing does it seem? Does it seem like proof of our conjecture?"

James said, "I think it will always work because you just take two numbers, add them together, and then you can always take 1 off of one number and put it onto the other number, and it will always be the same thing, for sure."

I was glad to hear this exchange. Jackson's initial representations a few sessions ago had not shown the relationship between expressions, but now he was clear about what Melody's representation showed. And James, who two sessions earlier had said it was impossible to prove a conjecture for all numbers, was now making a bold claim about his classmates' model.

Yet, I still wasn't sure where the class as a whole stood. Would some students be satisfied that testing many specific examples is sufficient proof? Did some students still think they would need to test more examples? Did they understand what it means to make an argument for all numbers? What did it mean to them when Melody said, "We don't know how many cubes are on the stick?" I needed to continue listening to the discussion with these questions in mind.

I next asked Maria and Anna to share their story problem. They had struggled with their representation, and I thought the class could work together to make their context clearer.

Maria read their story, "There are two parties. At one party, there are some people. At the other there are some. When an amount of people leave the party and go to the other, you will always get the same amount of people you started with, if you're adding the two parties."

The class felt the wording was awkward and wanted to clarify what was happening with the two parties. Paul suggested naming the parties, Party One and Party Two: "Some people from Party One go over to Party Two. There are still the same amount of people in all."

Isabel said, "Maybe you could say, there's like 50 people at one party and 30 people at another party, and 3 people from the party that had 30 people went over to the party that had 50, and then it was 27 + 53."

This was an important juncture in the conversation. With Isabel's suggestion that we insert specific numbers, I could learn more about where students stood with the idea of proof. Would they be satisfied that it works in general because it works in specific instances? Or would they see the power of saying "an amount of people"?

Eleanor said, "I think what Isabel said works, but it's not as general."

Ezra added, "I think it shows our conjecture more without numbers, because our conjecture doesn't actually mention any numbers. So we can't prove it if we just say one number."

We continued to discuss other representations. For each, I made sure we addressed the same core questions:

- How does the representation show addition?

- How does it show the two addends?

- How does it show one addend decreasing by some amount and one addend increasing by the same amount?

- How does it show that the sum must remain the same?

I also posed questions that addressed the nature of proof of a generalization:

- Does the representation show a specific instance of the conjecture or does it show it for all numbers?

- Does the representation convince us that the conjecture is true?

The students were engaged throughout the discussion and were interested in seeing their classmates' work.

Toward the end of the lesson, I asked the class to reflect on the set of representations we had looked at. Isaac said, "If we only had one thing to share to convince someone, I'm not sure the stories with numbers would prove it. We'd need something a lot more general."

Anna added, "I'm glad some of the representations made an exact number, like with the parties, and some for all numbers, like with Melody's cubes. We had different ways to think about it."

Latesha concluded, "If we all did something that was not general, then we wouldn't know what the general would look like."

By the end of the lesson, the class felt satisfied. I felt satisfied, too. It's not necessarily the case that every student would be able to devise a proof working alone, but all of the students were engaged in the discussion, could identify what the different representations showed, and considered the question of what it means to prove a claim for an infinite class of numbers. At the same time, all of the students have a firm understanding of the particular generalization—that as long as we stay in the realm of positive whole numbers, for any addition expression, if one addend increases by some amount and the other addend decreases by that same amount, the sum remains the same.

But our explorations do not end here. Do my students recognize that this generalization applies to addition and no other operation? That is where we'll go next—to look at the operation of subtraction to see if the same number patterns hold.

### *Commentary: Constructing Arguments*

Proving a general claim is a new endeavor for most elementary students, and the task needs to be presented in a way that makes sense to them. Ms. Fried began this phase of the teaching model by asking her students to think about large numbers, the largest numbers they could think of: Would their conjecture work? How did they know? She gave her students time to mull over those questions between sessions before they were charged with constructing proofs. Then she asked them to use representations—story contexts, cubes, or drawings—to explain to someone who hadn't been a part of their conversation that the conjecture must be true, no matter what numbers they chose.

As students took on the challenge, Ms. Fried remained alert to who understood the task and who was confused. She decided to devote an additional session to small-group time to assure that all students would have a solid footing as they entered the whole-group discussion. By putting students in groups of six for this session, they had a chance to practice explaining their arguments and got to listen to other pairs. Those students who were struggling had time to focus on one or two of their classmates' arguments, an opportunity to make sense of the idea of creating a proof in general terms.

Although many of the students created appropriate representations, the teacher did not take for granted that they understood the distinction between offering specific cases as supporting evidence and proving a general claim. Precisely because one of the students suggested that they use specific numbers to provide clarity, the class had an opportunity to discuss this issue, and the teacher had an opportunity to track what different students thought about this question.

The goal of the lesson was to have students understand some aspects of the nature of proof, though different aspects would sink in for different students. Some students might understand logical implication (that one thing causes another thing to happen); others might understand that a single example isn't a proof; and some students might understand the importance of using an example as a way of testing or trying to follow a proof, even if it's not the actual proof. Taking note of where students were at the end of this phase of the model, Ms. Fried had ideas of who was thinking largely in terms of specific numbers, who was using representations to show "any number," and who was moving between the two. She would use this information to make decisions about how to provide support when the class would return to proving in their investigation of the next conjecture.

.................................................................................

In the following video, the teacher poses a set of questions to the class to introduce the idea of proof.

**❙ FOCUS QUESTION**

**VIDEO 4.5** How do the teacher's questions about large numbers move students into ideas of proof?

.................................................................

Video 4.5 ▶

http://hein.pub/WDIW4.5

## PHASE V: COMPARING OPERATIONS

*Once students have verified a claim, they consider the question, "Does this work for other operations?" Returning to Phase I, students consider a set of problems, equations, or expressions that illustrate an analogous claim for another operation. They then go on to Phases II through IV to examine and prove a conjecture about the second operation.*

At this phase of the model, the class moves through the first four phases again but now considers a contrasting generalization analogous to the first but with a different operation. Even when students are convinced that their arguments are strong and valid, their work on a particular generalization is not yet over. Students often assume that their generalizations work with any *numbers,* but they don't focus on the fact that generalizations are specific to an *operation.* Having students explore a generalization about addition and then consider whether the same number pattern holds for subtraction or multiplication brings the operation to the forefront.

Before continuing to read the example, take time to explore the next generalization for yourself.

### MATHEMATICAL INVESTIGATION

Examine this set of expressions.

| | |
|---|---|
| 17 + 5<br>18 + 4 | 17 − 5<br>18 − 4 |
| 19 + 3<br>20 + 2 | 19 − 3<br>20 − 2 |

Look at the list of subtraction expressions compared to the list of addition expressions. What is changing from one expression to the next? What is the effect on the sum in the first column and on the difference in the second column?

What can you say about why making the same kind of changes in the subtraction expressions has a different effect on the result than with the list of addition expressions?

Can you make a list of related subtraction expressions that *do* have the same difference? Start with 17 − 5. List some equivalent expressions.

What generalization can be made about equivalent subtraction expressions? Write out your statement. Using counters, a drawing, a number line, or a story context, explain why your generalization must be true, no matter what subtraction expression you start with.

In the following account, look for how the teacher:

- highlights differences between operations as students move through the phases of the model, this time focusing on subtraction

- reminds students of what they learned about each phase of the work the first time through

- asks students, at the end of the lesson sequence, to reflect on the differences between the operations and between their conjecture about addition and their conjecture about subtraction.

Exploration of a generalization about equivalent subtraction expressions begins with a process similar to that of the exploration of equivalent addition expressions, with students noticing patterns in sequences of expressions. However, now they consider a set of subtraction expressions in contrast to a set of addition expressions. How do the two sets differ? What are implications for the conjecture they would propose?

### Ms. Fried's Class: Comparing Operations—Noticing Regularity and Articulating a Claim

At the end of our investigation of equivalent addition expressions, I saw that all of the students were able to hold onto the fact that our conjecture had two groups, that one group was getting larger by the same amount, that the other was getting smaller, and that sum of the two groups was unchanged. But for some students, the operation of addition seemed to be invisible. There were students who talked about two piles of sand and said you could move some scoops from one pile to the other and you still have the same sand you started with. But when I asked them where the addition part is in their story, they never talked about combining the piles. I was very curious about how they would respond to the question I posed to begin their work on contrasting subtraction with addition. After reading the class conjecture about addition aloud to the class—*If you have two addends, and you take away some amount from an addend and add the same amount to the other addend, it should equal the same sum*—I asked, "Do you think the same thing will happen when we subtract?"

I didn't ask for responses yet. I first provided a list of expressions with the same pattern they had examined for addition.

$$17 - 5$$
$$18 - 4$$
$$19 - 3$$
$$20 - 2$$

I pointed out that from one expression to the next, the first number increased by 1 and the second number decreased by 1. "What do you think?" I asked. "Is the same thing happening?"

When we recorded the differences, students realized that something else altogether was happening.

$$17 - 5 = 12$$

$$18 - 4 = 14$$

$$19 - 3 = 16$$

$$20 - 2 = 18$$

...................................................................................

**Adam:** Uh-oh. I thought the answers were going to be the same.

**Sage:** That's what I thought, too.

**Adam:** So I guess it only works for adding, not subtracting.

...................................................................................

Once they realized that what they expected was contradicted, I asked, "Is there something else that works for subtracting? Let's say we start with $17 - 5 = 12$. How can we change the numbers just a bit to find another subtraction expression equal to 12?"

The class soon came up with a list of expressions equivalent to $17 - 5$. Many of them had noticed this pattern before in their computation work but had never stopped to think about it beyond seeing the pattern of the numbers. All of the following expressions are equal to 12.

$$17 - 5$$

$$18 - 6$$

$$19 - 5$$

$$20 - 4$$

For the rest of the lesson, students worked in pairs to come up with more examples of equivalent subtraction expressions. Since the students were now familiar with the nature of the work, they were already coming up with language to describe the patterns they noticed before I presented the task to write a conjecture.

In the next lesson, we went through the same process we'd done with addition, having students work individually and in pairs to write a statement, and then editing a small set of the statements to create a class conjecture. At the end, our conjecture read as follows: *If you're doing subtraction, you can make both numbers go up by 1 or both numbers go down by 1, and you get the same difference.*

During the discussion, I spent some time clarifying the term *difference*, so that students would understand that it refers to the answer to a subtraction problem, just as *sum* refers to the answer to an addition problem. I chose not to introduce the terms *minuend* and *subtrahend*, because it takes so much effort to remember which term refers to the first number and which refers to the second. I didn't think the technical language would be helpful.

Although students were able to formulate a conjecture from the pattern of numbers, I felt students were generally less sure of what was going on in subtraction than they had been with addition. Combining two quantities was easier to picture than keeping track of the parts and whole when separating, removing, or comparing quantities. Even though I usually use small numbers in these sessions so that students can focus on structure rather than computing, I decided to present a problem with large numbers to see if they believed their new conjecture would apply.

I presented the equation $632 - 499 = \underline{\quad} - 500$ and said, "The question is whether the missing number would be 631 or 633."

................................................................

**Thomas:** I think it's $632 - 499 = 631 - 500$, because I think that, but I also have a gut feeling that the other one might work, too.

**Dede:** I think that it's $632 - 499 = 633 - 500$ because our rule says either both numbers have to go up or both numbers have to go down if you want to get the same difference.

................................................................

I wasn't sure if everyone agreed that the conjecture would apply here, and so I chose to voice that question: "Maybe our rule doesn't work for big numbers. Maybe it just works for small numbers." Sometimes I choose to put out an incorrect idea so that the class has an opportunity to consider it and challenge it. It's through such discussions that incomplete or confused ideas can be clarified. In this case, all the students who spoke up in response to my suggestion stated that the rule should work for these numbers, too.

................................................................

**Dede:** I think it works for all numbers, just like addition did.

**Nancy:** I think it's 633 because if it was addition, it would be 631.

**Thomas:** I'm rethinking now that I was wrong. I think it's 633.

**Sage:** Both numbers need to go up in subtraction or both numbers need to go down. If you higher one number and lower one number, that would be in addition.

................................................................

Although all those who spoke were convinced of their conjecture, I still sensed hesitation in the room. I didn't want to go rolling along with the assumption that everyone understood. Even the students who had spoken with assurance weren't offering reasons to support their assertions that referred to the structure of subtraction. As we ended the lesson, I wanted to assure those who were feeling uncertain and said, "Even though we have our conjecture, it seems to me that it's really difficult to visualize and explain how to make these equivalent expressions in a way that makes sense to all of us. In the next few Algebra and Proof lessons, we're going to work on representations, just like we did for addition, to find ways to explain why our conjecture is true and to prove whether it works for any numbers. Then I think we should come back to these larger numbers to see what we think."

### Commentary: Comparing Operations—Noticing Regularity and Articulating Claim

Although the students had explicitly written into their first conjecture that it applied to addition, they were surprised to realize that when they applied the same pattern to subtraction (increase one number in the expression by 1 and decrease the other by 1), the difference changed. By contrasting addition with another operation, they come to see that each operation behaves differently, leading to different patterns.

This time, when students were asked to state a generalization about subtraction, with their background of having created a generalization about addition, they had a better idea of what the articulation task involved. Once they realized that they needed to take a second look at the patterns in subtraction, they fairly easily formulated a conjecture: that the numbers in a subtraction expression must both increase or decrease by 1 in order to maintain the same difference. (In a later session, they would think through whether the numbers could increase or decrease by any amount, as long as the amounts are the same.)

However, even though they could notice and describe the pattern, the teacher sensed that students were more hesitant in the discussion. Subtraction is more difficult to visualize than addition: When thinking of subtraction as separating or removing, students must keep track of the whole, the part that's removed, and the part that remains. When thinking of subtraction as comparison, they must keep track of the two quantities being compared and their difference.

In the next phases of the teaching model, students investigate the effect of changes in the numbers of a subtraction expression on the difference through creating and manipulating representations of subtraction. They uncover the structure of subtraction and analyze *why* their conjecture works. At the same time, students continue to learn about what constitutes mathematical argument.

..................................................................

In the following video, students have come up with lists of equivalent subtraction expressions and have now come together to share their ideas. After viewing the clip, consider the focus questions.

### FOCUS QUESTIONS

Video 4.6 ▶
http://hein.pub/WDIW4.6

**VIDEO 4.6**   What do the students notice about the two lists of expressions? How does the teacher help students describe the number patterns they're seeing? How does the teacher make the transition between noticing patterns and making a conjecture? How do the students' initial conjectures reflect what they've noticed? How does the teacher support students to clarify their conjectures? Why might she ask students to clarify Abigail's conjecture?

..................................................................

In this next clip of another classroom, students review statements of their conjecture. Prior to the episode seen in the clip, students worked on their conjecture using their own language. Then the teacher introduced mathematical terms for the parts of the subtraction equation.

## FOCUS QUESTIONS

Video 4.7 ▶

http://hein.pub/WDIW4.7

**VIDEO 4.7**   Why might the teacher have introduced the mathematical terms? In what ways might these words be useful for the students? In what ways might they get in the way of students' thinking?

What idea does Giancarly contribute to the discussion of the class conjecture?

### Ms. Fried's Class: Comparing Operations—Investigating with Representations and Constructing Arguments

For many of my students, it took a while to see how to create a representation that would demonstrate the conjecture. All of my students could show subtraction with cubes or a number line, and they could all create a subtraction story. But it was more of a challenge to transform their representation to show how one expression is equivalent to another.

For those students who were creating story contexts, it was hard for them to think of a context in which the difference remains the same. I was thinking a good problem might involve the ages of two people. If you think about the difference between your age and that of your mother, a year from now the difference will be the same, even though your ages changed. But the stories my students created weren't in terms of subtraction as comparison. Instead, they were thinking of subtraction as removal.

For example, Ezra and James were thinking about chicken wings. You have 17 chicken wings and then the dog comes and eats 5 of them. There are 12 chicken wings left. How would the story change so that you subtract $18 - 6$? Why would you need to maintain the same difference? In the end, they decided they were having a party and needed 12 chicken wings. However many chicken wings they started with, the dog knew it could eat some but had to leave 12. When they put more chicken wings in the refrigerator, those were chicken wings the dog could eat.

Maria and Latesha came up with a story about a boy holding helium balloons. If he holds more than 12 balloons, he'll float away. So he starts with 17 balloons and quickly has to pop 5. If he starts with one more balloon (18), he has to pop an additional balloon (6), in order not to have more than 12.

Two pairs of students used number lines to represent the problems. Kim and Mike showed subtraction as movement to the left. They showed $17 - 5$ by starting at 17 and moving back 5.

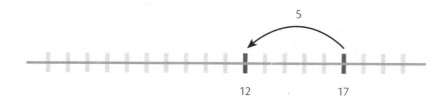

They struggled for a while about how to show adding 1 to the 17 and adding 1 to the 5, but once they drew 18 − 6, they realized they had just that.

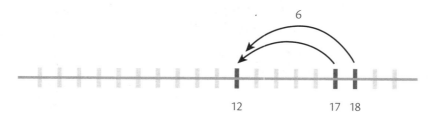

Kim said, "I can see it now. If I start 1 ahead, at 18, but I go back 1 more, I land at the same place."

Alice and Denise used a number line, too, but showed subtraction differently. In their number line, the difference, 12, is shown as the distance between 5 and 17.

When they added 1 to each of the numbers of the subtraction expression, the line that designated the difference shifted over one space. The difference, shown by the length of the line, stays the same.

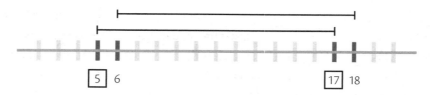

Kim, Mike, Alice, and Denise finished their number lines while the rest of the pairs were still creating their representations, so I put the two pairs together and asked them to see if they could all make sense of both representations.

The same distinction appeared in the cube representations different pairs created. Dede and Nancy showed 17 − 5 as removal. They started with 17 cubes—12 blue (shown as dark gray) and 5 green (shown as light gray). When the 5 green cubes are removed, the 12 blue cubes are left. But when they started with the 17 cubes and added 1 white cube to make 18, they subtracted the 6 green *and* white cubes, and were still left with 12. The white cube represents an increase of 1 both to the total number of cubes and to the amount removed, that is, 17 − 5 becomes 18 − 6.

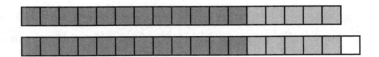

On the other hand, Thomas and Adam showed a stack of 17 cubes and a stack of 5 cubes. 17 − 5 is shown as the difference between the two stacks.

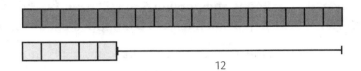

When they added 1 cube to each stack, representing 18 − 6, the difference between the stacks was unchanged.

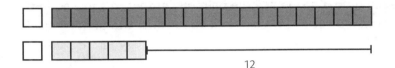

As I did with the pairs who created number lines, I put Thomas and Adam together with Nancy and Dede to share their representations.

For the whole-group discussion, I planned to start with story contexts. I often choose to start that way because the stories allow many students to more easily keep track of the components of the problem. For example, we can talk about the chicken wings that were put in the refrigerator, those the dog ate, and those left for the party. Then we can use cubes to illustrate the context. Dede and Nancy's representation directly mapped onto the chicken wing or balloon stories.

The discussion of students' representations took several of our 20-minute Algebra and Proof sessions. For each representation, I stayed focused on these core questions:

- How does the representation show subtraction?

- How does the representation show the amount we started with?

- How does the representation show the amount that is subtracted?

- Where do we see the difference?

- How do you see the numbers in the subtraction expressions increasing by 1?

- Where do you see that the difference stays the same?

For the first several representations, we worked with 17 − 5 and 18 − 6, but once the class seemed solid with how those quantities appeared in the representations, I started working with different numbers. What if the expressions were 13 − 6 and 14 − 7? How would the representation change? What if they were 25 − 2 and 26 − 3?

We were working with Latesha and Maria's problem context about the balloons when I decided this would be a good time to extend the generalization further. By this point, several students had mentioned, over the course of our investigation into subtraction, that the change could be 2 or 3 or some other number. I had put off bringing up this idea to the whole class until I thought more students had developed representations that helped them make sense of the change of 1.

.........................................................................................

**Ms. Fried:** So this picture that Latesha and Maria made about the balloons shows that the boy had 17 balloons and popped 5 to still have 12, then 18 balloons and popped 6. Those little explosion lines are the popped balloons, right, Latesha?

**Latesha:** Right. Every time you add another balloon, it has to be popped, so both numbers keep going up by 1, but he's always still got 12.

**Ms. Fried:** Here's my question. Our conjecture now says, "If you're doing subtraction, you can make both numbers go up by 1 or both numbers go down by 1, and you get the same difference." This picture shows the amounts changing by 1 each time. Can we use the balloon context to show adding or subtracting an amount that's not 1? Turn and talk about this, and then I'll ask for your ideas.

.........................................................................................

After a few minutes of time in pairs, I brought the group together.

.........................................................................................

**Ms. Fried:** Who has an idea about how to use the balloon story to show that we can change our subtraction expression by other numbers and still have the same answer, the same difference?

**Ezra:** He has 17, he has to pop 5, like we said. But it doesn't just have to go up by 1. Give him 100 more; then he has 117, so he has to pop 100 more.

**Ms. Fried:** So how many does he have to pop?

**Isaac:** He has to pop 105. 117 take away 105 is the same as 17 take away 5.

**Roberta:** It could be 1017 and 1005.

**Maria:** He'd have to pop 1005. He'd have to do it really fast.

**James:** The more balloons you give him, the more he has to pop. That's why both numbers keep going up.

**Sage:** And they have to go up by the same amount. If you higher the first number, you have to higher the second number, or you won't get back to the same answer.

.........................................................................................

With that idea in mind, I suggested we look back at our class conjecture. Is there anything they'd like to change? In the next session, I made time for the class to work individually and in small groups before we considered possible statements in whole group. By the end of the discussion, the class had revised the conjecture to read:

> *If you're doing subtraction, you can change the first number and the second number by the same amount and you get the same difference. You can add an amount*

*or subtract an amount, but you have to do the same thing to both numbers or you won't get the same answer.*

### Commentary: Comparing Operations—Investigating with Representations and Constructing Arguments

In the representing phase, the teacher is supporting students not only in their attempts to show the transformation of the subtraction expressions but also in understanding the different representations. While students were working in pairs, Ms. Fried kept track of who created what kind of representation—whether they were using story contexts, number lines, or manipulatives—and also whether they were thinking of subtraction as removal or comparison. Some of what makes subtraction more challenging than addition is that there are different ways to interpret it. In Ms. Fried's class, most of the students represented subtraction as removal, but two pairs created representations that showed subtraction as comparison.

Knowing that the class discussion would start with story contexts that represented subtraction as removal, Ms. Fried made sure all students were oriented ahead of time. That is, those students who had created representations that showed subtraction as comparison had time to examine and discuss at least one pair's representation that showed subtraction as removal.

In that way, everyone could focus on the important idea: What in each representation corresponded to the components of the conjecture? Whether they were focused on specific numbers or were making arguments for the general case, students explained how they saw subtraction and how the subtraction expressions were transformed while maintaining the same difference.

Now that the class had discussed the variety of representations, constructed arguments for why adding 1 to each number in a subtraction expression produces an equivalent expression, and extended the generalization to adding or subtracting any amount to the numbers, Ms. Fried was ready to turn back to addition so that her students could consider both conjectures together.

.......................................................................................

In this video clip, students have created representations of their subtraction conjecture. In addition to cube representations, students created the following story contexts:

*A boat can hold only 12 people or it will sink. If 15 people are on it, 3 people have to get off. When more people get on the boat, that number of people will also have to get off.*

*Alyssa has 15 cookies but she needs only 12, so Kussita ate 3. If Alyssa gets more cookies, Kussita will eat more.*

**❙ FOCUS QUESTIONS ❙**

**VIDEO 4.8, SECTION 1** How do the three representations—the cubes, the boat story, and the cookie story—map onto each other?

How does the teacher draw students' attention to these connections?

Video 4.8 ▶

http://hein.pub/WDIW4.8

**VIDEO 4.8, SECTION 2**   What does the teacher do to help students consider how the representation can be used to think about a sequence of subtraction expressions equal to 12?

.................................................................

### Ms. Fried's Class: Comparing Addition and Subtraction

To conclude the Same Sum, Same Difference sequence, I asked the class to read our two conjectures.

> *If you have two addends and you take away some amount from an addend and add the same amount to the other addend, it should equal the same sum.*

> *If you're doing subtraction, you can change the first number and the second number by the same amount and you get the same difference. You can add an amount or subtract an amount, but you have to do the same thing to both numbers or you won't get the same answer.*

Now that we had been deep in the territory of subtraction, I wanted all their hard work on addition to become present for them again. I also wanted them to see clearly and distinctly how addition and subtraction are different. I was curious about what was on their minds, so after having a student read each of the conjectures aloud, I asked for comments without a focusing question.

Adam asked whether we were going to check out the patterns with multiplication and division. Jason thought maybe, since multiplication is like addition and division is like subtraction, we would need only two rules for the four operations. I told them we would have a chance to explore multiplication and division later in the year, and asked again what they were thinking about the work we had done on addition and subtraction.

Eleanor said, "When you're adding, you keep the same stuff, just move it around. It's different for subtracting."

I asked the class, "What's different when you changed subtraction expressions?"

Ezra said, "You bring in more stuff, so you have to take away more stuff."

A few more students offered ideas, and then Sage summed up the feelings of the class: "When we got the idea of seeing if our addition rule works for subtraction, I was like, of course it works. And then it was like uh-oh, it doesn't work, and I lost all hope. I'm happy we found a very close but different rule."

### Concluding Commentary

This discussion in which students reflect on their work of the last weeks illustrates their investment in the ideas. Having explored generalizations for equivalent addition and subtraction expressions, they are curious about what happens with multiplication and division. Jason shares his expectations based on hunches he has about what is similar and different about the operations. Perhaps you can investigate what makes equivalent multiplication expressions and what makes equivalent division expressions. In what ways is Jason's thinking on track, and what does he have yet to figure out?

The students' comments also demonstrate that they are emotionally involved in this work. Sage describes how she *lost all hope* when what she expected proved false and *was happy* the class found a close but different rule. What has happened that Ms. Fried's students are so invested in mathematical ideas?

First and foremost, Ms. Fried gave students' ideas center stage. She invited students to share their thinking and listened hard to what they offered. Because she set up the expectation that students attend to the ideas of their classmates and build ideas together—and demonstrated such careful attention herself—students took their own and their classmates' ideas seriously. They knew they were doing important mathematics.

Indeed, over the course of a semester, working two or three days a week, 15 to 20 minutes per session, the class has traveled far—from noticing symbol patterns across expressions, to formulating conjectures, to representing the conjecture and constructing arguments that explain why the conjecture must be true for all whole numbers. The surprise they felt when they realized the symbol patterns that worked so beautifully for addition did not work for subtraction took them into another investigation. The second time through the process, they understood what they were after and felt greater confidence about what it means to make a representation-based argument in mathematics.

Ms. Fried did not rush students to come to an argument. She recognized that each phase of the teaching model has a focus and a purpose. At each phase, she invited students to voice their ideas and did not assume the discussion was over because one student stated a claim, had a representation that worked, or presented an argument. She understood the productivity of lingering. Probing through the use of core questions, she allowed students to present a variety of ideas, wording suggestions, and representations. It is in making connections across ideas, word choices, and representations that concepts are strengthened.

## CHAPTER FOCUS QUESTIONS

*Use these questions to think back over Chapter 4 as a whole, including the classroom examples and video clips.*

1. Thinking back on the chapter as a whole, what are two or three of the teachers' moves that strike you as critical in supporting the students' development of ideas? Refer to specific text or video examples.

2. How did teachers support the participation of the range of students in their classrooms? Refer to specific text or video examples.

3. Throughout the sequences, teachers invite students to share their thinking and, at the same time, focus students' attention on aspects of the content that will move the discussion forward. That is, teachers contain the discussion so that it doesn't spin out or become chaotic. Reviewing the text and video examples in this chapter, look for particular moves made by the teachers that illustrate opening up the discussions to student thinking or constraining the discussion to maintain focus.

4. Review the questions the teachers ask in each phase of the investigation. What are one or two of the kinds of teacher questions and actions you noticed in this chapter that you think would be useful for you to practice in your own classroom?

# 5

# Mathematical Argument
# in the Elementary Classroom:
# Impact on Students and Teachers

Even though mathematical argument has become more prominent in the current discourse about mathematics teaching and learning, many teachers, teacher educators, and school leaders may still have questions about what students learn. In this final chapter, we share what we've learned about what students gain from engaging in this work. Our evidence of student learning comes from written assessments we administered to the students in the collaborating classrooms, teachers' written accounts, extensive classroom observations, and student interviews.

Integrating the phases of mathematical argument into content that is fundamental in the elementary grades supports students' learning in multiple ways. We'll examine what students gained in the following three categories:

- mathematics content and practices

- applying new understandings in students' regular mathematics work

- participation and confidence among the range of learners.

## MATHEMATICS CONTENT AND PRACTICES

From our written assessments, we found that students who regularly participated in lessons like those in the lesson sequences scored significantly higher on items that emphasized explanation and argument, interpreting expressions and equations, and understanding the structure of the operations than those who did not. The assessment problems were constructed to encourage mathematical reasoning and to focus on structure. For example, students were asked to determine whether the equation $27 - 9 + 9 = 27$ is true or false and to correctly complete the equation $35 + 12 = 25 + \underline{\phantom{..}}$ and to explain their answers. Although these problems can be solved by computing, students who had participated in the collaborating classrooms did not simply compute an answer but drew on their knowledge of mathematical relationships, structures, and properties to solve them and could justify their reasoning. For example, for the first equation students who use mathematical reasoning, or what has been termed *relational thinking* (Carpenter et al. 2005), recognize that subtracting an amount, then adding the same amount, is equivalent to adding zero. In the second problem, students can solve the problem by using the idea that subtracting an amount from one addend and adding the same amount to another addend creates an equivalent expression. Students were also asked to write a story problem for a given number sentence, such as $12 - 3 = \underline{\phantom{..}}$ or $6 \times 8 = \underline{\phantom{..}}$. Being able to contextualize the quantities and operation shows that students understand how the quantities are related, given that operation.

Beyond these written assessments, and perhaps even more important, is what we saw in classroom observation and documentation. Four key areas of learning math content and practices, described next, emerged as students engaged in lessons on mathematical argument. The quotations are from collaborating teachers' reflections at the end of the school year.

### Noticing Regularities and Making Conjectures

As students were repeatedly asked to notice patterns in sets of related problems, equations, or expressions, they became better attuned to what patterns might be interesting mathematically. Teachers noted that by the spring semester, more students were taking the initiative in noticing patterns and wondering whether a pattern holds. One teacher commented, "I think that the students have learned that there are patterns and connections with math. . . . If we can start them off noticing from a young age, it will become a routine in itself and something they can then carry with them throughout their math classes." Another wrote: "My students are definitely noticing a lot more in math. They are looking for patterns with numbers. They are a lot more inquisitive. They also are making conjectures in regular math class. Our conjecture board grew as the year went on because they were constantly trying to come up with conjectures."

### Engaging in Mathematical Reasoning

Students learned to dig into a mathematical idea in depth. As one teacher commented, "One very powerful result has been the expectation that mathematical ideas are something to reason about, and that there are regularities to look for and notice within our computation work." Spending an entire semester on one set of related ideas allowed students time to have initial ideas, interact with their classmates around those ideas, revisit and revise their thinking, and use the time between sessions for the ideas to percolate.

They learned what it means to use representations to construct a mathematical argument: "In analyzing rules and making claims, I think that most students have a much better understanding that you can't make a claim based on a number of examples that fit what you are trying to prove. Most students understand that you must be able to generalize the claim and create a representation that shows the claim working for any numbers." Teachers noted that the class discussions were critical in this work. Together students built on each other's ideas to come up with representation-based arguments they would not have been able to construct individually.

### Recognizing That the Operations Have Meaning, Properties, and Behaviors

Many elementary students encounter an operation like addition or subtraction only as a directive to carry out a certain action and find a result, rather than as an object that can be described. They don't think of an operation as having certain properties and behaviors (e.g., how increasing the amount that's subtracted from a number *decreases* the difference, while in adding two numbers, increasing the second addend *increases* the sum). Through their work on mathematical argument about the operations, students learn how each operation is different from the others. This understanding of how operations function is fundamental to mathematics, not only in the elementary grades as students work with whole numbers, fractions, and decimals, but also in later years as they make sense of new classes of numbers, such as integers, and of algebraic expressions. One teacher observed, "During these sessions, [students] are required to work on one concept and really investigate it. Even when something is familiar to them, they have to look at it more closely and notice the behaviors of addition and subtraction or multiplication and division." Teachers noted that both they and their students focused more on the meanings of the operations in math class: "I used to feel like students learned one way of, say, multiplying, and then I would show them how to multiply differently when they were introduced to fractions and decimals. Now students are thinking of multiplying as something that stays the same and looking for the ways it plays out with new classes of numbers."

### Developing Mathematical Language

In the course of noticing patterns, articulating conjectures, and constructing mathematical arguments, students are repeatedly placed in the position of trying to make their ideas clear to their classmates. They learn that something that may be completely clear to them has to be explained with precision, with specific references to parts of expressions and corresponding parts of representations, in order for others to understand an idea. A teacher commented, "I hadn't expected to be as interested in hearing and interpreting students' attempts at making claims or even how they describe a comparison between two equations. Working through and fine-tuning their articulations has helped them get clearer about their ideas and has helped me learn more about what they may or may not understand." The focus on making ideas clear so that they can be examined also provides the opportunity for teachers to introduce useful mathematics terms into the conversation: "Repeated exposure to mathematical vocabulary not only allows students to talk about their ideas but, for many students, it also allows them to understand the ideas that are being discussed. Of all the useful skills students have acquired as a result of these sequences in mathematics instruction this year, consistent use of mathematical vocabulary for discussing, explaining, or inquiring about topics has had a particularly dramatic impact on student understanding."

## APPLYING NEW UNDERSTANDINGS IN STUDENTS' REGULAR MATH WORK

Students applied what they learned in the lesson sequences to their core curriculum in two ways: noticing and making conjectures, and applying generalizations about the operations to solve problems.

### Noticing and Making Conjectures

Teachers found that after developing the habits of noticing patterns and regularities, students extended those habits to regular math instruction as they articulated conjectures about the mathematics they were studying. For example, in one class working with division, a student noticed that if a number is divisible by another number, it is also divisible by factors of that number: 81 is divisible by 9; it is also divisible by 3, which is a factor of 9. The student who made this observation was not yet making a generalization; he was noticing that this was true for particular numbers. But students began to wonder if his idea would always be true. Recognizing the importance of this idea mathematically, the teacher asked students to investigate by creating representations. They were soon busy building models and trying out further examples.

Teachers also noted that students would bring in ideas they had worked on independently, like one third-grade girl who noticed on a homework page that $2 \times 8 = 16$, $1 \times 8 = 8$, and $\frac{1}{2} \times 8 = 4$. She thought that maybe $8 \times 1\frac{1}{2}$ would be 12, because the answers "should count by 4s, and there should be something in between 8 and 16." A teacher wrote, "During our regular math instruction we spent time noticing and discussing patterns we may not have paid any attention to prior to our Algebra and Proof work. Students used language like, 'I can prove they're related!' and 'Let's write a conjecture for that!'" Another commented, "As the year goes on, the 'noticing' becomes more valuable, and they begin to do it on their own more. We might be looking at a series of story problems and someone might point out that the equations we created are related, or they immediately tell the subtraction equation that is related to addition problems we are working on."

### Applying Generalizations to Solve Problems

Students also used the conjectures they had studied in the Mathematical Argument lessons to solve problems during their regular math instruction. Although students had used some of these strategies in the past, teachers noticed that they brought to their application a new depth of knowledge about which strategies might work and why they worked. For example, a teacher wrote, "We are working on three-digit addition, and many students are comfortable using equivalent expressions for friendlier starting points. In the past I typically had only a few students who would be comfortable using equivalent expressions as a strategy or taking from one addend temporarily to make it friendlier and then adding that amount back at the end. Now, many students do this on their own." Another commented, "I noticed that after children participated in [these] sessions, they were much more likely to catch answers that didn't make sense in regular math class. . . . 'This is just like our conjecture,' was something I heard about our study of multiplication." A third teacher summed up the application to regular math work in this way: "In our regular instruction, we do a lot of work around strategies for solving problems. The [mathematical argument] work gave them a much deeper understanding of why those strategies work."

## PARTICIPATION AND CONFIDENCE AMONG THE RANGE OF LEARNERS

As part of the project's focus on the education of all learners, project staff and teachers observed and discussed who was participating in the students' discussions, how they were participating, and whether there was room in these discussions for all students to contribute ideas. What were students who generally excelled in grade-level computation learning from these lessons? What were students who had a history of difficulty with grade-level computation learning?

Overall, we saw increased substantive participation across the school year. The nature of the discussions invited students to offer just one thing they noticed, one aspect of a pattern, or a few words to start the articulation of a conjecture. Because the answers to equations being considered were already known, students weren't as concerned about being wrong. A teacher wrote, "There were many more ways to participate than offering an answer, most of which children viewed as less risky than being 'wrong.' Children could look for patterns, think about other examples that supported a claim, restate ideas in their own words, or think of examples that might not work." Because ideas were analyzed and revisited over the course of many short lessons, students had time to become familiar with them, make them their own, and learn to ask their own questions. Further, the development of the ideas was situated not in individuals but in the community, allowing broad ownership and contribution. "Someone would throw out an idea and others would then add on," one teacher said. "Sometimes the language was hard to unscramble, but they all felt confident just to contribute even if it only started the conjecture. This really carried into regular math class. Students who were timid and shy seemed to find their voice after we worked in the Math Argument sessions."

One teacher commented on some of her students who entered the school year with lower confidence in mathematics: "Students who were less engaged during math at the beginning of the year (and classified themselves as bad at math) came out of their shells and truly engaged in mathematical discussions! They like math now and have changed their perception of themselves as math students. Also, many of the students who had difficulty explaining their thinking early on in the year are very capable of it now, and the sense of pride that they exude fills me with great joy." Another added, "So frequently kids who struggle in math are taught the tricks and very specific ways to solve problems. I feel that this work benefited them in that they were really able to dive into the operations. They were able to witness how the operations function, and this helped to propel them forward in their thinking." Teachers also noted how their students who have little difficulty with grade-level mathematics participated in this work: "Watching my 'advanced' math students struggle to show their ideas in pictures, or be very specific in their wording of a claim, made me realize that this work is challenging for all kinds of learners. Perhaps this was because students could follow what seemed most interesting and accessible to them wherever they were in their math development."

Through the "productive lingering" we described in Chapter 1, students have the opportunity to participate, as a community of mathematicians, in substantive mathematical investigation. Sustaining work on a few related generalizations over a whole semester allows students to investigate mathematics deeply, as another teacher noted: "Since these lesson sequences focus on one particular concept over a few months, or about twenty sessions, it allows all of the students to really dig in to their learning. There are so many opportunities for the struggling students to continue to work on their ideas, and at the same time the more advanced students can continue to push themselves to think further about a particular concept, representation, [or] conjecture."

The ongoing, short, focused sessions, two or three times a week, allowed for breathing room, time between sessions for students to reflect, consolidate, and come up with further ideas and questions. For example, one teacher observed that when she kept the sessions short, more students participated. If she kept going because a few students had more ideas, or because she herself became intrigued with an idea, only the students who had more to say participated. In order to go further, many students need time to let ideas settle. Allowing this time for students to mull over ideas was important to keep everyone engaged. Productive lingering doesn't mean simply letting discussions go on and on. It involves going beyond the superficial acceptance of a proposed idea by giving it focus within a lesson, providing time to mull it over between lessons, and revisiting the idea in order to deepen knowledge over multiples lessons.

## MATHEMATICAL ARGUMENT: AN OPPORTUNITY FOR TEACHER LEARNING ABOUT FUNDAMENTAL MATHEMATICS

Not only did we see impact on students, we also found that the focus on mathematical argument engages elementary teachers in learning more about what mathematics is and what it means to do mathematics. Collaborating teachers reported that implementing the teaching model and the lesson sequences in their classrooms provided a framework that helped them reflect on their teaching practice, particularly in the following three areas:

- questioning

- attending to student thinking

- understanding mathematics as a discipline.

Using the core questions and other suggested questions in the sequences, teachers built up what one teacher called a "bank of questions" to help push students' thinking. A teacher commented, "My questions improved with time. I knew better what questions to ask and how to frame them. By the spring, I was more discerning about which questions to ask when."

Asking good questions is closely tied to attending carefully to student thinking, even when that thinking at first seems muddled. Teachers learned to listen for and take advantage of the patterns and regularities students noticed during their math work. A teacher wrote, "I continue to learn what it means to listen and to balance my agenda for moving ideas forward with listening fully to what my students have to say. I have learned to have more confidence in their ideas, even when they may initially seem off the mark." Teachers commented on the central importance of class discussions as vehicles for clarifying and extending math ideas. "I have learned that children can build bigger ideas together as a group than individually," said one teacher. "Participating in this project reinforced for me how important dialogue is in the classroom. Often, I could watch ideas forming as we talked together."

Teachers improved their own knowledge of mathematical argument. According to one teacher, "I have learned so much. From the basics of just learning that these general claims exist to how to make a proof! I learned to feel more confident in my ability to struggle through and try and make sense of things that I would have thought far too hard before." Teachers also noted changes in their own approach to students and to what constitutes significant mathematical activity. One wrote, "I learned to be careful about how I define success in mathematics. I call positive attention when students take risks in sharing unfinished thoughts, raise questions, listen to peers and build on their ideas, speak up when they're feeling stuck or confused, or share an interesting idea or representation. Although I continued activities involving computational fluency, we spent many discussions talking about how this skill is only one piece of the puzzle and that if you have a deep understanding of concepts, you can apply this to solve any problem." Through learning about the five phases of the teaching model and implementing the lesson sequences, teachers have the opportunity both to learn about mathematical argument for themselves and to integrate this important practice into their instruction. In this project, as in others we have worked on over the years, we find that elementary teachers, given the opportunity, are engaged by serious mathematics and tenacious in learning what might initially seem to them difficult and unfamiliar.

Both students and teachers who participated in these lessons came to understand that they were undertaking significant mathematical work and attempting to say something "big" about what is true in mathematics. As Ms. Kent's student, Rose, said in Chapter 3, "These are not just everyday ideas that you come up with every day." Teachers learned that elementary students could engage in these ideas and did so with energy and focus, taking on substantive and satisfying mathematical investigations. In the words of our collaborating teachers, "My students were so curious, and I wonder if they just never had an opportunity to think in this way. . . . Instead of lessons that we were teaching, it felt like much more of a journey that we were on with the students." We hope this book and the accompanying lesson sequences provide a framework, tools, and the encouragement for others to take that journey in their own classrooms.

# APPENDICES

. . . . . . . . . . . . . . . . . .

## About the Lesson Sequences

The Lesson Sequences on Mathematical Argument are designed to support teachers in bringing the ideas of mathematical argument to students in grades 2 to 5. There are eight sequences: two in this appendix and all available as an online resource (see page 87).

A sequence offers a set of activities built around the teaching model described in this book. Each lesson sequence explores two to three related general claims in twenty to twenty-five lessons. Each lesson is intended to be 15 to 20 minutes long. Field-test teachers implemented two sequences each year, one in the first half of the year and one in the second half of the year.

Field-test teachers used different parts of the school day to work on the sequences. Some integrated the lessons into their morning meeting time; others worked on them just before or after lunch; still others linked them to their regular math class. Doing a sequence effectively requires two to three sessions each week, so that continuity can be maintained.

The following pages list for each sequence its name, the general claims it explores, in what book chapter it is referenced (if any), and the recommended grade levels. Choosing sequences to work with will depend on your students' mathematics experiences. The sequences that involve addition and subtraction might be used at any grade, while those that involve multiplication and division can be used after students have developed some familiarity with those operations.

The lesson sequences are intended to be a flexible framework that teachers can shape in response to their own students' ideas and the pace of their work. Field-test teachers often stretched a single lesson over several sessions. The lessons are not a curriculum but a structure that guides you and your students through the five phases of the teaching model.

## SEQUENCE 1 Core Ideas of Addition and Subtraction (Whole Numbers) [CAS]

- Claims Investigated

  » Changing the order of the addends in an addition expression does not change their sum. Includes work with two and three addends.

  » Changing the order of the numbers in a subtraction expression changes the difference except when the two numbers are the same.

  » Addition and subtraction are inversely related.

- Illustrated in Chapter 1

- Recommended Grades: 2–5

## SEQUENCE 2 Changing a Number in Addition or Subtraction (Whole Numbers) [CNAS]

- Claims Investigated

  » In an addition expression, if 1 (or some amount) is added to an addend, the sum increases by 1 (or that amount).

  » In a subtraction expression, if 1 is added to the starting amount, the difference increases by 1.

  » In a subtraction expression, if 1 is added to the amount taken away, the difference decreases by 1.

- Illustrated in Chapter 1

- Recommended Grades: 2–5

## SEQUENCE 3 Same Sum, Same Difference (Whole Numbers) [SSSD]

(See Appendix A)

- Claims Investigated

  » In an addition expression, if you add an amount to one addend and subtract the same amount from another addend, their sum remains the same.

  » In a subtraction expression, if you increase (or decrease) both numbers by the same amount, their difference remains the same.

- Illustrated in Chapter 4

- Recommended Grades: 2–5

### SEQUENCE 4 Core Ideas of Multiplication and Division (Whole Numbers) [CMD]

- Claims Investigated

  » Changing the order of the factors in a multiplication expression does not change the product. Includes work with two and three factors.

  » Changing the order of the numbers in a division expression changes the quotient, except when the two numbers are the same.

  » Multiplication and division are inversely related.

- Recommended Grades: 3–5

### SEQUENCE 5 Changing a Number in Addition or Multiplication (Whole Numbers) [CNAM]

(See Appendix B)

- Claims Investigated

  » In an addition expression, if you add some amount to an addend, the sum increases by that amount.

  » In a multiplication expression with two factors, if you add 1 to a factor, the product increases by the other factor.

  » In a multiplication expression with two factors, if you add some amount to a factor, the product increases by the other factor multiplied by that amount.

- Illustrated in Chapter 3
- Recommended Grades: 3–5

### SEQUENCE 6 Factors, Products, and Fractions (Whole Numbers and Fractions) [FPF]

**Note:** *Sequence 6 extends ideas that are explored in Sequence 5. Students should complete that sequence before beginning this one.*

- Claims Investigated

  » In an addition expression, if you add some amount to an addend, the sum increases by that amount.

  » In a multiplication expression with two (positive) factors:

    ▪ If the factors are both greater than 1, the product is greater than both of the factors.

- If one of the factors is equal to 1, the product is equal to the other factor.

- If one of the factors is equal to 0, the product is equal to 0.

- If one of the factors is between 0 and 1, the product is less than the other factor (unless the other factor is 0).

» In a whole-number multiplication expression with two factors, if you add a fraction to one of the factors, the product increases by the other factor multiplied by the fraction.

- Illustrated in Chapter 2

- Recommended Grades: 4–5

### SEQUENCE 7 Same Product, Same Quotient (Whole Numbers) [SPSQ]

- Claims Investigated

  » In a multiplication expression, if you multiply one factor by an amount (not equal to 0) and divide the other factor by the same amount, their product remains the same.

  » In a division expression, if you multiply (or divide) the dividend and divisor by the same amount (not equal to 0), their quotient remains the same.

- Recommended Grades: 3–5

### SEQUENCE 8 Multiplication, Division, and Powers of Ten (Whole Numbers and Decimals) [MDPT]

- Claims Investigated

  » When a number is multiplied by 10, every digit moves one place to the left.

  » When a number is divided by 10, every digit moves one place to the right.

  » If you multiply a number by a multiple of 10, for example 20 or 30, you multiply that number by the number of tens, for example 2 for 20 or 3 or 30, then move all the digits one place higher.

- Recommended Grades: 4–5

### *But Why Does It Work?* Online Sequences

To access the online resources for *But Why Does It Work?*, please go to www.heinemann.com
and click the link in the upper right to **Log In**.
(If you do not already have an account with Heinemann,
you will need to create an account.)

Register your product by entering the code: **WDIW.**

Once you have registered your product,
it will appear in the list of **My Online Resources**.

# Same Sum, Same Difference (Whole Numbers) [SSSD]

**Grade Range:**  Suggested for grades 3, 4, or 5

**General Claims:**  In an addition expression, if you add an amount to one addend and subtract the same amount from another addend, their sum remains the same.

$$a + b = (a + n) + (b - n)$$

In a subtraction expression, if you increase (or decrease) both numbers by the same amount, their difference remains the same.

$$a - b = (a + n) - (b + n)$$

**Number of Sessions:**  Twenty-eight

**Teacher Notes**

1.  Students' Story Contexts for Equivalent Addition Expressions

2.  Representations of Equivalent Addition Expressions

3.  Representation-Based Argument for the Addition Claim

4.  Students' Story Contexts for Equivalent Subtraction Expressions

5.  Representations of Equivalent Subtraction Expressions

**6.** Representation-Based Argument for the Subtraction Claim

**7.** Algebraic Notation

**Student Sheets** to accompany the following sessions: 3, 17, 19, and 26

## Same Sum, Same Difference (Whole Numbers)

**General claims:**

1. In an addition expression, if you add an amount to one addend and subtract the same amount from another addend, their sum remains the same. For example, $6 + 9 = 5 + 10$ or $26 + 56 = 30 + 52$. Students will first consider the case in which 1 is added to one addend and subtracted from the other. In everyday language, students might state the conjecture this way:

    - If you take 1 from one number and add it onto the other number, you'll get the same answer you had before.

    - To have the same sum, you can break off one piece of one number and stick it onto the other number. If you do that, you will always have the same sum.

    - One of the numbers goes down and the other one goes up the same amount. Then you get the same sum.

    - When you're adding two amounts, if you take something off one addend and add that same amount onto the other addend, you get the same sum as you had the first time.

2. In a subtraction expression, if you increase (or decrease) both numbers by the same amount, their difference remains the same. For example, $9 - 6 = 10 - 7$ or $72 - 36 = 76 - 40$. Students will first consider the case in which 1 is added to both numbers. Students might state the conjecture this way:

    - When you are subtracting, if you add one more onto each of the numbers, you will get the same difference that you had the first time.

    - In subtraction, if you take an amount off of one number and take the same amount off the other number, you get the same difference (or you could add the same amount).

    - If you want to have the same difference, you can move both numbers up the same amount or move both numbers down the same amount.

    - You have to increase both the subtrahend and the minuend the same amount, and then you'll get the same difference.

You will want your students to come up with their own wording for the claims.

## Goals for Students

The lessons in this sequence provide opportunities to work on a range of mathematical issues, depending on the needs of individual students. Although all students will be engaged in the same activities, different students will take away different learnings. All students will be engaged in deepening their understanding of the properties and behaviors of addition and subtraction. While students have encountered addition and subtraction for a number of years, not all students have thought through how these operations work. Through investigating how equivalent expressions are related in these two operations, they deepen their understanding of what an operation is—not just a direction to solve problems but a mathematical object with particular characteristics. All students will benefit from the practice with addition and subtraction and with representing these operations in ways that strengthen their grasp of the nature of these operations. The particular claims with which students will be working can also be applied to computation, adding to the repertoire of calculation strategies students can rely on, and thereby increasing their flexibility and accuracy as they compute.

## Sequence Overview

The first eighteen sessions of the sequence focus on the claim about addition, Session 19 invites students to consider if the same claim is true for subtraction, and the remaining sessions focus on the subtraction claim.

Of the sessions focused on addition, the first nine provide opportunities for students to notice and articulate patterns within pairs of addition expressions; Sessions 10 through 16 offer opportunities for students to investigate specific instances of the addition claim with representations such as drawings, number lines, cubes, and story situations. After representing several specific instances of the claim, students work to represent the general case using the same representational tools, and then consider for what sets of numbers the claim is true. Sessions 17 and 18 provide opportunities for students to make connections between the claim and computational strategies.

The final set of sessions explore the same process but focus on subtraction. Students notice and articulate in Sessions 19 and 20; investigate specific instances with representations in Sessions 21 and 22; and work to make arguments about the general claim in Sessions 23 and 24. Then they consider for what sets of numbers the claim is true. Sessions 26 and 27 offer links between the claim and strategies for computation. The final session is an opportunity for students to summarize this sequence as they compare the behaviors of addition and subtraction relative to equivalent expressions.

One aspect of this work that is key to helping students develop their arguments is to periodically work at making explicit the links between the numerical expressions, the story situations, the cube models, the visual drawings or number lines, and the components of the claim written in words. Embedded in the sessions are core questions, which are designed to support making these connections across the representations, the number symbols, and the claim explicit. Even if it seems your students are making sense of the articulations of the claim and believe it to be true, asking the core questions helps students shift from a focus on what is happening with the numbers to noticing and articulating how the operation behaves.

Following the entire sequence of sessions allows students to fully investigate and make arguments for these claims using the set of whole numbers (0, 1, 2, 3, 4 . . .). Once a claim is established for the set of whole numbers, depending on grade level and experience, some classes might want to continue this work beyond the twenty-eight lessons to see how to modify the class claims or arguments to accommodate other kinds of numbers, such as fractions or integers.

SESSION **1** : **Noticing Regularity—Addition**

*Whole class; individuals or pairs*

"We're going to start doing some sessions in mathematics that aren't part of our regular math classes. In these sessions, we're going to be thinking about different things that can be said about addition and subtraction. We're going to try to figure out how to state clearly what our ideas are and how we can prove them. Because these sessions will be about generalizations and proving, we're going to call them 'Algebra and Proof sessions.'

"Today we're going to look at some addition expressions and think about some ways that addition works."

Post the following sequence:

$$1 + 14$$

$$2 + 13$$

$$3 + 12$$

$$4 + 11$$

"What do you notice about these expressions?"

Listen to what students offer. Continue to ask, "What else do you notice?" to encourage participation. Students often see the addends as being in two columns and say something like, "These numbers [in the first 'column'] go up, and these numbers [in the second 'column'] go down." If no one brings up that the sum of each expression is 15, ask, "What can you say about the sums?"

Ask, "Can you continue the list? What addition expression would come next? Then what would be the next one? How are you changing the addition each time?" When you get to 6 + 9 in the list, ask, "Is the sum still 15? How do you know?"

Show a cube train of 14 interconnecting cubes and a single cube. "Here I'm showing 1 plus 14. How could I change it to show 2 + 13? Now, how would I change it to show 3 + 12? What do you notice about what is happening?"

Continue adding on to the list of expressions, following students' suggestions. As students respond, draw attention to these ideas: (a) If you start with one expression in the list, the next expression has one number that increases by 1 and one number that decreases by 1; (b) each expression has a sum of 15.

Note: When you get to 7 + 8, the next expression is 8 + 7. Some students may wonder whether they should continue because they see 8 + 7 as the same as 7 + 8. They might say, "8 + 7. It's just the same numbers turned around, and all the rest will be the same ones we already have, just reversed." Acknowledge that they are noticing something important about addition, that reversing the order of the numbers doesn't change the sum. It is actually not critical whether you continue the list at this point. If you feel that your students have the idea of adding and subtracting 1, you can stop with 7 + 8. If they want to continue finishing the list, it's fine to complete it quickly.

Once the list is finished, ask, "Are these all the ways to make 15 with two addends? Can you think of any others?" Listen for students' ideas. If students have not already mentioned 0 + 15, they may add that now. "Does 0 + 15 fit in with your ideas about adding 1 and subtracting 1?" If some students bring up (–1) + 16, let them know that for this sequence, the class will work with just positive whole numbers.

Students now work individually or in pairs to generate expressions with two addends for 24.

For next session: Keep the list of expressions that make 15 posted. Students should bring their expressions that make 24 to Session 2.

## SESSION 2 : Noticing Regularity—Addition

*Whole class*

Students should have their list of expressions that make 24 with them. With the class, generate the list of pairs for 24. If your class as a whole easily generated the expressions in order (i.e., 0 + 24, 1 + 23, 2 + 22, . . .), you do not need to spend time ordering them. If quite a number of students did not put them in order, just ask for different expressions, and list them as they come up. Then ask the class whether there is a way to put them in order. Again, it is up to you and the class whether you continue the list after 12 + 12 to show all the expressions with the addends reversed.

Once the list is complete, ask, "What is the same about our list of expressions for 15 and our list of expressions for 24?"

Accept students' observations. Students may have a variety of observations— that all the expressions have two numbers and a plus sign, that the order of each expression can be reversed, that one number in each expression increases by 1 and one number decreases by 1, that the sum of all the expressions in each list is the same. Again, ask students to talk you through using cubes to demonstrate briefly how the expressions for 24 change. You might start with 10 + 14, change it to 11 + 13, and then to 12 + 12.

Remind students that these lessons are about proving ideas in mathematics. Let students know that they're going to be focusing on the idea about increasing one number by 1 and decreasing the other number by 1.

Post the following:

$$36 + 50 = 86$$
$$37 + 49 = \underline{\phantom{00}}$$

Discuss: How can you use the first problem to solve the second?

If needed, ask, "Can your idea about adding 1 and subtracting 1 help with this problem?"

For future sessions: Keep the lists of expressions with sums of 15 and 24 posted.

# SESSION 3: Noticing Regularity; Review of Equation Format

*Individuals, whole class*

Students work on the Session 3 Student Sheet.

For the last 5 minutes of the session, bring students together.

Post:

| | |
|---|---|
| 10 + 5 | 12 + 12 |
| 9 + 6 | 11 + 13 |

"What do you know about these pairs of expressions?"

Once students say that the expressions in each pair are equal, put an equal sign between the expressions in each pair. "You're saying 10 + 5 and 9 + 6 both equal 15, so I'm going to put an equal sign between them like this. What does it mean if I write 10 + 5 = 9 + 6?"

Use this opportunity to make sure students understand that the equal sign indicates that one expression is equivalent to the other. If students are inexperienced with this use of the equal sign, they may believe that it means "now write down the answer" and may not see it as a symbol that indicates equality. So some students may say, "You can't write it that way because 10 + 5 doesn't equal 9, it equals 15. That's wrong," or, simply, "That doesn't look right." Acknowledge students' confusion: "Why doesn't that look right?" At the same time, reinforce students' ideas about the equal sign showing the equality of the two expressions.

If the meaning of the equal sign seems familiar to most of your students, this can be just a quick review. If a number of students seem unfamiliar with the use of the equal sign, you may need to continue to revisit this discussion.

For the next session: Select some of the expressions students came up with for the second question on the Session 3 Student Sheet. Select those that illustrate adding 1 to an addend and subtracting 1 from the other addend. If a number of students generated examples in which they added and subtracted amounts other than 1, include some of these as examples.

---

1. Can you figure out which problems have the same sum without adding? Connect the ones with the same sum.

| | |
|---|---|
| 10 + 5 | 11 + 13 |
| 12 + 12 | 49 + 26 |
| 9 + 6 | 17 + 19 |
| 18 + 18 | 50 + 25 |

2. Write a problem that has the same sum as each of these problems. Can you do it without adding?

A.  9 + 11 _____

B.  20 + 30 _____

C.  14 + 16 _____

D.  19 + 19 _____

See page 126.

SESSION **4** : **Articulating a Conjecture**

*Whole class; individuals or pairs*

Post the pairs of expressions you selected from students' work on the second question from the Session 3 Student Sheet, for example:

$$9 + 11 = 10 + 10$$

$$14 + 16 = 15 + 15$$

$$19 + 19 = 18 + 20$$

$$14 + 16 = 12 + 18$$

$$20 + 30 = 25 + 25$$

Discuss briefly: How do you know these expressions are equal? How can you put into words what is going on?

Tell students that they are going to each write a general statement about what is happening with these pairs of problems. Their job is to write a statement that is as clear as possible so people who didn't know what they've been talking about would understand.

Students work individually or in pairs to write in their own words why the two expressions are equal. (Some students might write about adding and subtracting 1 while others might expand their idea to include adding and subtracting any amount.) While they write, circulate. If students ask for mathematical terms ("What's the answer called?"), provide them. You will go over these with the whole class in the next session.

Collect students' statements.

For the next session: Select four or five statements to post in the next session. It is likely that some of your students' statements will be similar, so choose examples that represent a range of wording choices and ideas, including statements that are clear and complete about adding and subtracting 1 resulting in the same sum (you may want to post several of these with different wording, so students can compare); statements that describe adding and subtracting 1 but do not mention what happens to the sum or do not indicate to what numbers the changes are made; statements that are vague about how much is added and subtracted; statements that are about adding two specific numbers; statements that indicate that amounts other than 1 can be added and subtracted; and so forth. Some examples in everyday language representing the range of responses follow:

- You add 1 and subtract 1.

- One number goes up, and the other goes down.

- $9 + 6$. I add 1 to the 9 and take away 1 from the 6. So it's $10 + 5$. And even though I change it, it would be the same answer.

- Add 1 to an addend and subtract 1 from the other addend, and you still have the same answer you had before.

- You can add an amount to one number and subtract that same amount. You still get the same sum.

Note: Using algebraic notation is not a focus of this sequence. However, some students may bring up ideas about notation. If any students have used algebraic notation to represent their conjecture, you can include that on the list if it is correct. See Teacher Note 7: Algebraic Notation for more information and guidance.

## SESSION 5 : Articulating a Conjecture

### Whole class

Post some of the students' rules from Session 4.

Introduce the word *conjecture*. A conjecture is a statement in mathematics that we think is true but has not been proved. "All of these statements are conjectures. We haven't yet proved that they are true for all numbers." Let the students know that you are now going to work on developing a clear class conjecture. "We need to be clear about what our conjecture is before we try to prove it."

The class looks at the statements you have listed. Read the various statements aloud. Which parts of the statements are especially useful or clear to students? One way to say this is: "Which of these statements, or parts of these statements, would help people who haven't been part of the work we've been doing so far understand our conjecture?"

After students have offered some ideas, draw their attention to the words *addend* and *sum*. "As I was watching you write your statements in the last session, some of you were trying to remember the mathematical words that are used for addition. Here are some mathematical terms that might be useful as we try to make our conjecture clear." Put up an addition statement, such as $6 + 9 = 15$, and make sure students can identify the addends and the sum.

Note: By third grade, students should be able to use the terms *addend* and *sum* in their conjecture. However, you might also want to have a statement of the class conjecture that uses more familiar language. That way, students can refer to the familiar wording (e.g., if you add 1 to one number and subtract 1 from the other number in addition, the answer doesn't change) while they are learning the mathematical terms.

Have students edit the statements to create one (or two) clear class conjecture(s). At this point, even if some students have come up with conjectures that involve adding and subtracting any amount, stick to adding and subtracting 1 for this conjecture. You can let students know that the class will return to the idea of adding and subtracting other amounts.

Once students are satisfied with their statement, have them use one of the familiar examples (e.g., $6 + 9 = 5 + 10$) to make sure they know what part of the equation is meant by each part of the statement of the conjecture.

Note: You may find that students continue to come up with improvements to make the conjecture clearer and more precise. You can continue considering revision of the conjecture as the sequence continues.

# SESSION **6** : Investigating with Representations

*Individuals or pairs*

Draw students' attention to the class conjecture(s) and to this list of expressions:

$$4 + 20 = 24$$

$$5 + 19 = 24$$

$$6 + 18 = 24$$

"Our class has made a conjecture about addition, but we haven't proved it yet. In the next few sessions, we're going to be investigating whether this conjecture is always true and whether it is true for all numbers, not just the ones we've tried. Today I'd like you to start to think about how our claim works and why it's true. Here are three of the expressions that make 24."

"To help us understand what is happening, I'd like you to write a story problem for $4 + 20$. Then, change the story just enough so that it is about $5 + 19$. Then change it just enough again so that it is about $6 + 18$. As you're writing, think about how your stories help show why the sum stays the same when you add 1 to one addend and subtract 1 from the other addend. Can your stories help show *how* this works and *why* this has to be true?"

Students work in pairs or individually to write their stories. As students work, circulate and think about which stories to share in the next session.

Note: There are several types of stories to look for. See Teacher Note 1: Students' Story Contexts for Equivalent Addition Expressions for more information about these types and how to select stories to share in the next session.

SESSIONS **7-8** : **Investigating with Representations**

*Whole class*

Share some of the story problems students created in Session 6. For each set of stories, ask these core questions:

- How do the stories show addition?

- How do they show how the addends change?

- How do they show what happens to the sum?

As students talk, illustrate with quick sketches what they are saying about how the addends change, so that all students have images of the stories, not just the words.

For example, for a story about cats up in a tree and on the ground, you might sketch a tree with 4 small circles ("cats") on it and 20 small circles next to it ("on the ground"). Then, as students talk about how a cat moves from the ground to the tree, you can cross out 1 of the circles on the ground, show with an arrow how it moves to the tree, and draw it in a different color (so that it can be distinguished from the 4 cats already there) on the tree.

Note: In many classes, some story contexts have emerged as particularly useful for the class to consider as they work on proving their claim. Look for whether one or two of the story contexts seem to be especially powerful for many students in understanding the relationship between the changes in the addends and the value of the sum.

SESSION **9** : **Articulating a Conjecture—For Which Numbers Does Our Conjecture Work?**

*Whole class*

Review the class conjecture. If further suggested edits have come up, you can consider them now.

Note: If students suggest that the claim could be about adding and subtracting any amount, not just about adding and subtracting 1, ask for numerical examples of what they mean. Record their examples and conjecture, but leave the conjecture(s) about adding and subtracting 1 in place. Let students know that you'll come back to this idea. However, most students will need to work through proving the conjecture about adding and subtracting 1 first.

Ask:

"What numbers does this conjecture work for?"

"Will it work for numbers that are larger than what we've been using in our problems?"

"Will it work for really large numbers? How do you know? What's the largest number that you think will work?"

Ask for and record examples as students respond. Pose follow-up questions to probe whether your students think of positive whole numbers as an infinite class. For example, depending on their responses, follow-up questions can include:

"What do you mean by 'any number' (or 'all numbers')?"

"What's the largest numbers you think our conjecture will work for?"

"What do you mean by 'infinity'?"

"What do you mean 'the numbers go on forever'?"

Note: Some students may mention fractions or negative numbers. For example, one student said, "You can take a fraction away from one fraction and add it onto the other fraction, and you would still have the same sum." Accept these comments, and indicate how interesting it is that they are thinking about other types of numbers. You might record these ideas as questions: "Does our conjecture work for fractions?" In this sequence, you will focus only on whole numbers (positive integers and 0). Once they have developed an argument for all whole numbers, and depending on grade level and experience with the concepts of fractions or integers, some students might enjoy the challenge of investigating how to modify their representations to accommodate other numbers.

SESSIONS **10-11**: **Investigating with Representations/Proving the Conjecture**

*Whole class; individuals or pairs*

Review students' discussion in the last session (modify the following depending on what your students said): "Most of you seem pretty convinced that our conjecture is true for all numbers, at least the whole numbers that go from 0 up to very large numbers. Some of you say the numbers go on forever.

"But we've tried out our conjecture with only a few examples, like our charts for 15 and 24. How do you know that our conjecture is true for any numbers? What if someone said that maybe there are some examples when it wouldn't work? How could we know for sure?"

Ask, "Would we have to show this for every addition expression separately to prove our conjecture? Or is there some way to show that our conjecture would be true, no matter what the addends are?"

Note: Some students might say, "It works for the cases we tried, so it must always be true." This does not constitute proof in mathematics. Other students might say, "We can't possibly try every example because the numbers go on forever, so we can't say if it will always be true." These students realize that it's not enough to say that if it works a few times, it must always be true. They understand that there might be numbers that they haven't tested yet for which the conjecture doesn't work, and they have a sense of numbers (or, at least, the counting numbers) as infinite. These students are articulating something important about mathematics. However, they believe the only way to determine if something is true about the operations is to perform the calculation and see if it comes out right. Therefore, they believe, one can never make a claim about an infinite set, like all whole numbers. This is an important stage of learning. It is likely your class will include students with a range of beliefs about mathematical argument. The next set of lessons is designed to support students in developing mathematical arguments.

"Today I'd like you to work on proving our conjecture. I'd like you to start by using some kind of representation to prove that a new example works. Then some of you might want to see if you can figure out a way to use your representations—your picture or cubes or number line—to figure out how to prove our conjecture for any numbers."

Post:

$$23 + 9 = 22 + 10$$

$$14 + 6 = 15 + 5$$

To focus students on the purpose of these representations, you might say something like, "You can choose one of these examples. These are easy numbers for you to add. I know you can figure out that the sum of $23 + 9$ equals the sum of $22 + 10$. But here's the challenge: What I want you to do with some kind of representation is to show *why* if 1 is added to one addend and subtracted from another addend, the sum *has to* stay the same. Why is our class conjecture true? Why does it work? If you add 1 to 9 and subtract 1 from 23, does it have to be that the sum is still 32? How could you show that it has to work that way?"

Review with the class what they might use for representations: They might draw a picture (they can use $X$s or circles or squares, for example, to represent the quantities), use connecting cubes, or draw jumps on a number line; or they could make a picture of one of their story contexts by drawing or with cubes. If there are story contexts that have been particularly salient for your class and have the potential of being generalizable, you can specifically suggest those. (For more information, see Teacher Note 1: Students' Story Contexts for Equivalent Addition Expressions, and Teacher Note 2: Representations of Equivalent Addition Expressions.)

"You can show how and why our conjecture works with these specific numbers. Then, if you want to, you can see if you can use your representation to show why it has to work that way with any addends."

Note: It is likely that students won't finish (or perhaps won't even start) their representations in Session 10 but will need to continue and complete them in Session 11. However, encourage students to be efficient in making their representation. Their pictures and models need to show what is happening without being overly elaborate (e.g., if they are using the cats story, they don't need to draw individual cats; a cube or a square or an $X$ can represent a cat). However, color can be important in making their representation clear. For example, students might consider using different colors for the two addends, or showing what is changing or moving by using color.

For the next session: Select several of the students' representations to share with the whole class. Look for a variety of representations—pictures, cube models, and number lines, as well as illustrations of story contexts. Identify both representations that show the specific numbers of the examples and representations that show more general arguments.

## SESSIONS 12–13 : Investigating with Representations, Proving the Conjecture

### Whole class

Remind students that now the class is working on finding a way to prove whether their conjecture is true. Start with representations that use specific numbers. Make sure that a range of representations (cubes, pictures of a story context, other pictures, number line) is illustrated.

For each, make sure it is clear to students what the two expressions are; write them so that the students see them with the representation. For each representation, ask the following core questions:

- How does this show addition?

- How does it show 1 being added and subtracted?

- How does it show that the sum stays the same?

- Does it represent the claim to you? How?

If some students are using more general language (e.g., "any amount") for their representation, next share these. Ask the core questions:

- How does this show addition?

- How does it show 1 being added and subtracted?

- How does it show that the sum stays the same?

- How does it represent adding any two numbers?

- Does it represent the claim to you? How?

If no students are using more general language yet, choose one or two of the representations that have potential to be generalizable. For each, ask students, "Is there a way you can talk about this representation without using specific numbers?" You may want to give them a way to start: "Could you talk about one of the representations in a different way, for example, 'There were some cats in a tree and some cats on the ground.'" Or you might say, "Could you talk about this cube model without saying how many cubes are in each stick? For example, you could start, 'There are some red cubes in a stick and some blue cubes in another stick.'" Then ask, "Could anyone keep going with this idea and show us with one of the representations how our conjecture works no matter what the addends?"

For example, some students might say, "It doesn't matter how many cats are in the tree and how many cats are on the ground. If 1 cat moves from the ground to the tree, then there is 1 more cat in the tree and 1 less on the ground, but it's still the same number of cats. No cats ran away." Or, "See, if I move a blue cube from here to the red stick, it's just moving—it's not changing anything. I could have a million blue cubes and a million red cubes. It doesn't matter. I'm just moving a cube over. The number of cubes isn't changing." These students understand that they can make a claim about all numbers because this is the way addition has to work. (See Teacher Note 3: Representation-Based Argument for the Addition Claim.) Such a statement would constitute a convincing argument.

Ask other students to comment on whether these arguments are convincing. If students say that the amount added and subtracted can be any amount, not just 1, work on revising the articulation of the claim. If not, bring this up in the next session.

SESSIONS $14$-$15$ : **Expanding the Conjecture/ Claim and Investigating the Expanded Conjecture with Representations**

*Whole class; individuals or pairs*

If students have not previously developed a conjecture that the amount added and subtracted can be any amount, not just 1, pose a problem for students to consider:

$$46 + 98$$

**Can you come up with an equivalent problem that's easier to solve?**

Students have come up with 44 + 100, 40 + 104, and 50 + 94 and could explain how these can be solved easily mentally (for the last, students thought of it as 50 + 50 + 44, adding 50 + 50 first, then adding on the 44). Ask students to explain how they know the problems they propose will result in the same sum.

Then have students work on writing a conjecture about adding and subtracting amounts other than 1. Or, if students had previously articulated this conjecture, review it with the class.

Now present the task for them to work on individually or in pairs: "How can you adapt one of the representations we used to prove our conjecture about adding and subtracting 1 to now prove that we can add and subtract any amount? Choose one of the representations we used—it can be your own or someone else's—cubes, a picture, a number line, or a representation of one of our story contexts—to show why this new conjecture is true. You can use your representation to show either specific numbers or to show 'any number.'

## SESSION 16 : Investigating the Expanded Conjecture with Representations

*Whole class*

Share a few representations of the expanded claim.
Ask these core questions about each:

- How does this show addition?
- How does it show that the addends can be any numbers?
- How does it show that any amount can be added and subtracted?
- How does it show that the sum stays the same?
- Does it represent the claim to you? How?

## SESSION 17 : Application

*Whole class; individuals or pairs*

Pose this problem:

$$399 + 234$$

**"What's a problem that has the same sum but is easier to solve by using our claim?"**

Note: While it may be obvious to some of your students that an equivalent, easier problem is 400 + 233, not all students are always fluent with adding 1 to 399; they get stuck at moving from the 3 hundreds into the 4 hundreds. If this comes up for your students, you may want to work further on these kinds of problems (e.g., 399 + 1, 399 + 2, 298 + 4, 195 + 10) in your regular math class as well.

Record as: 399 + 234 = 400 + 233.

Say something like, "You can use our conjecture to make some addition problems easier to solve. Look at the problems on this sheet. Choose at least three that you think will be easy to solve by applying our claims, and write down the equivalent problem you would use for each one. Choose at least three that you would solve another way. Be ready to say why you chose the ones you'd solve using or not using our conjecture and why."

Students work individually or in pairs on the Session 17 Student Sheet.

---

1. Find at least three of these problems that you would solve using the class conjecture about adding to one addend and subtracting from the other. Show how you would change the problem to make it easier to solve.

2. Find at least three of these problems you would solve a different way. Be ready to explain your choices.

| | | |
|---|---|---|
| 25 + 75 | 99 + 9 | 49 + 51 |
| 19 + 36 | 26 + 34 | 87 + 36 |
| 45 + 63 | 90 + 70 | 229 + 56 |
| 99 + 99 + 99 | | |

See page 127.

SESSION **18** : **Application**

*Whole class*

Discuss the problems from Session 17. Students should have their own work from the last session.

"What are examples of problems you'd solve by using our claim about addition to make an easier problem? What are examples of problems you would solve in some other way?"

This discussion can be lively. Students may disagree on which problems they would solve by adding 1 (or some amount) to one addend and subtracting 1 (or the same amount) from the other addend and which problems they would solve in other ways. This makes sense because different students are comfortable with different strategies and with fluency in adding and subtracting to transform problems. Students may also point out that a combination of strategies can be useful.

The points to be made here are that: (1) looking at a problem as a whole before you try to solve it can help you pick a strategy appropriate for that problem; (2) transforming a problem into an equivalent, easier problem can be a very useful strategy, but you need to evaluate whether it helps in a particular case; (3) there are indications that might help you choose when to use this strategy—for example, if one of the addends is close to a multiple of 10 (let students suggest other tips); (4) no one strategy is best for all problems; what really helps with computation is to have several strategies you can rely on and apply as appropriate.

SESSION **19** : **Comparing Operations/Noticing Regularity: Subtraction**

*Whole class, then individuals or pairs*

Draw attention to your addition conjectures/claims.

"Does the same thing happen with subtraction? What if you add 1 to the first number and subtract 1 from the second number in a subtraction expression? Do you get the same difference?"

"Let's try a few. How about $17 - 5$?"

With students, generate a list of three or four expressions by adding 1 to the first number and subtracting 1 from the second number:

$$17 - 5$$

$$18 - 4$$

$$19 - 3$$

$$20 - 2$$

"Turn and talk to a partner. Is the same thing happening with subtraction as happened when we added and subtracted 1 in addition problems?"

"I'm hearing a lot of you say it isn't working. When you change the problem in the same way we changed addition problems, you *don't* get the same answer. So, here's the question. How *do* you get equivalent subtraction expressions? The answer to $17 - 5$ is 12. Suppose we want our answer to always be 12 and you can use only subtraction? Can you change $17 - 5$ just a little so that the answer is still 12?"

Explain that the student sheet contains some starting expressions. Their job is to come up with other subtraction expressions that equal 12 by changing the starting expression a little bit, and then changing the next expression a little, and so on. On the back, they can write any conjectures they have about getting the same answer in subtraction.

Students work individually or in pairs on the Session 19 Student Sheet.

For the next session: (a) Select a few of the students' sequences of equivalent expressions to post. Select several that show adding 1 to or subtracting 1 from both numbers. If some students made sequences in which a number other than 1 is added and subtracted, you can show one or two of those as well. However, keep in mind that most students may need to work thoroughly with the idea of adding or subtracting 1 before they are ready to think about adding/subtracting other amounts; (b) select a number of the students' conjectures to share. Look for conjectures about adding 1 to both numbers or subtracting 1 from both numbers. Again, if some students have written about adding or subtracting any amount, you can also include examples of those.

1. Starting problem:         $17 - 5$

   Build off that:         _____

   Build off that:         _____

   Build off that:         _____

2. Starting problem:         $20 - 18$

   Build off that:         _____

   Build off that:         _____

   Build off that:         _____

3. Starting problem:         $25 - 5$

   Build off that:         _____

   Build off that:         _____

   Build off that:         _____

See page 128.

# SESSION 20 : Noticing Regularity/Articulating a Conjecture

## Whole class

Put up some sequences from students' work on the Session 19 Student Sheet, for example:

| | |
|---|---|
| $17 - 5$ | $17 - 5$ |
| $16 - 4$ | $18 - 6$ |
| $15 - 3$ | $19 - 7$ |
| $14 - 2$ | $20 - 8$ |

Some of the sequences may add 1 to both numbers while others may subtract 1. Some students may also have experimented with adding or subtracting other amounts.

"Here are some of the sequences of subtraction problems with the same answer. What do you notice about these subtraction expressions?"

After students have made a few observations, read aloud a selection of conjectures they wrote on the Session 19 Student Sheet. Which parts of the statements are especially useful or clear to them? One way to say this is: "Which of these statements, or parts of these statements, would help people who haven't been part of the work we've been doing so far understand our conjecture?"

Have students edit the statements to create one (or two) clear class conjecture(s) about adding (or subtracting) 1 to both numbers in a subtraction problem.

Note: You can introduce *minuend* (the starting amount), *subtrahend* (the amount subtracted), and *difference*, but don't push these terms. *Difference* may be more useful than the other two terms, which are easily confused. Students can decide when and whether to use these terms. As before, if some students want to use the math terms as part of the conjecture, you might want to have two statements of the conjecture, one with the math terms and one that uses more familiar language.

If some students have come up with conjectures that involve adding and subtracting any amount, you can write a conjecture about that as well. If students have some ideas about this but aren't yet ready to formulate a conjecture, you can let them know that the class will return to the idea of adding and subtracting other amounts.

Once students are satisfied with their statement(s), have them use one of the examples you posted (e.g., $17 - 5 = 18 - 6$) to make sure they know what part of the equation is meant by each part of the statement of the conjecture.

You may find that students continue to come up with improvements to make the conjecture clearer and more precise. You can continue considering revision of the conjecture as the sequence continues.

SESSIONS 21-22 : **Investigating Through Representation**

*Individuals or pairs*

Introduce this task by saying something like this: "You've come up with a conjecture (or conjectures) about subtraction. Just like we did for addition, we're going to start working on seeing if we can prove that it's true by using pictures, models, and stories to represent what is happening and why it is happening. Today you will be making up a story context for two subtraction expressions and creating a representation to show how those two expressions are related—how the numbers in the problem change and what happens to the difference. Try to think of a story context—it can be a funny one or a fantasy one—where the difference *has to stay the same* when the two numbers in the expression change. Keep in mind that eventually we'll be seeing if we can prove that our conjecture is true for any numbers. So you might want to think about making up a story and creating a picture that later we can use for any numbers."

Explain that their task is to create a story context for $15 - 3$, then change it just enough to make the story about $16 - 4$ and to make a representation—cubes or a picture or a number line—to show how some of the numbers are changing but the difference stays the same. Remind them to try to think of a reason that the difference has to stay the same in their story.

To focus students on the purpose of these representations, you might say something similar to what you said when they represented the addition conjecture: "I know that these are easy numbers for you to subtract, and we already know that the difference for both expressions is 12. But the challenge is to use your story to show *why* if 1 is added to both numbers, the difference *has to* stay the same. Why is our class conjecture true? Why does it work? If you add 1 to the 15 and add 1 to the 3, does it have to be that the difference is still 12? How can you use a story context to show that it has to work that way?"

As students work, circulate and ask them to explain what they are showing with their representation. If they are representing specific numbers, have them explain what they are doing. If they seem ready to consider questions about the general claim, ask, "Is there a way you could use your picture/model to talk about 'any number'? For example, instead of saying, 'This stack of cubes shows the 15 mice,' could you start by saying something like, 'This stack of cubes is some number of mice'?" If they are trying to develop a general argument, remember that a representation-based argument involves both the representation itself and the explanation of the representation. Encourage students to develop the words that make clear what is represented by each part of their picture or model.

For the next session: Choose a few representations to share in the next session. Try to include an example of each kind of representation your students use: a picture, cubes, a number line. Think about which representations have the potential to be generalizable to "any numbers." See Teacher Note 4: Students' Story Contexts for Equivalent Subtraction Expressions, and Teacher Note 5: Representations of Equivalent Subtraction Expressions.

SESSIONS **23-24** : **Investigating Through Representation**

### Whole class

Share a few of the stories with their representations.

Remind students that now the class is working toward finding a way to prove whether their conjecture is true, but that they are starting by representing how their conjecture works with specific numbers. Make sure that a range of representations is illustrated.

For each, make sure it is clear to students what the two expressions are; write them so that the students see them with the representation. In the first of these two sessions, for each story and representation, ask the following core questions:

- How does this show subtraction?

- How does it show 1 being added to (or subtracted from) each number in the problem?

- How does it show that the difference stays the same?

- Does it represent the claim to you? How?

For the second of these two sessions, choose two or three stories and representations that have the most potential for generalization. First, review the conjecture the students are working on. Then, for each representation, make sure that students are following how the representation shows the claim in terms of its specific numbers (if that needs to be reviewed from the previous session). Then ask:

Is there a way to use this story and representation to show that our conjecture is true for any numbers?

Note: If students do not seem ready for this question, you might first ask, "How would I have to change this representation to show that 26 + 24 is equal to 25 + 25?"

You may want to give students a way to start: "Could you talk about one of the representations in a different way, for example, 'There was some number of mice, and the cat ate some of them; she saved the rest for her kittens; the next day there was 1 more mouse. . . .'" Or you might say, "Could you talk about this cube model without saying how many cubes you are starting with and how many you are taking away? You could start, 'There are some cubes in a stick, and then I take some away; if I have a stick that has 1 more cube . . .'" Then ask, "Could anyone keep going with this idea and show us with one of the representations how our conjecture works no matter what the two numbers in the problem are?"

Students might say, "If the cat has to save a certain number of mice for her kittens, then every time there is 1 more mouse, the cat can eat that one. So if the number of mice goes up by 1, the number eaten goes up by 1, too. If it goes up by 1 more, then she can eat 1 more. And it just keeps going. The more mice, the more she can eat." Or, "See, this stack of red cubes and blue cubes. It could be any number of red cubes and any number of blue cubes. If I take away the blue cubes, I always have the red cubes left. If I always want to end up with that number of red cubes, then every time I put an extra blue cube on, I have to subtract all the blue cubes I already had plus that 1 more. The more cubes I have to start, the more I have to take away. If I have a million extra blue cubes to start, then I have to take away a million more cubes." These students understand that they can make a claim about all numbers because this is the way subtraction has to work. (See Teacher Note 6: Representation-Based Argument for the Subtraction Claim.) Ask other students to comment on whether these arguments are convincing.

Note: If you think students are ready to consider the following question, or if this idea has already come up from your students, you might also ask:

Does our claim work only for adding 1 to (or subtracting 1 from) the numbers in the problem? Could we add other amounts, like 2 or 10 or some other amount? What would happen to the difference?

SESSION **25**  **Considering the Domain: For Which Numbers Does Our Claim Work?**

*Whole class*

Review the class conjecture. If further suggested edits have come up, you can consider them now.

Note: If students suggest that the claim could be about adding (or subtracting) the same amount from both numbers, not just about adding (or subtracting) 1, ask for numerical examples of what they mean. Record their examples and conjecture, but also leave the conjecture(s) about adding and subtracting 1 in place.

Focus students' attention on the conjecture about adding (subtracting) 1:

What numbers does this conjecture work for?

Will it work for numbers that are larger than what we've been using in our problems?

Will it work for really large numbers? How do you know? What's the largest number that you think will work?

Ask for and record examples as students respond. Pose follow-up questions to probe whether your students think of whole numbers as an infinite class. For example, depending on their responses, follow-up questions can include:

What do you mean by "any number" (or "all numbers")?

What's the largest numbers you think our conjecture will work for?

What do you mean by "infinity"?

What do you mean, "the numbers go on forever"?

Note: Some students may mention fractions or negative numbers. For example, one student said, "You can add a fraction, like $\frac{1}{2}$, to both numbers, and you would still get the same difference. Like if I have $5 - 3 = 2$, then $5\frac{1}{2} - 3\frac{1}{2}$ still equals 2." Accept these comments and indicate how interesting it is that they are thinking about other types of numbers. You might record these ideas as questions: "Does our conjecture/claim work for fractions?" However, keep the focus of this session on developing an argument for whole numbers. Once arguments are made for whole numbers, depending on grade level and experience with concepts of fractions or integers, some students might want to extend this work by investigating how to modify the arguments to accommodate other kinds of numbers.

SESSION **26** Application

*Whole class; individuals or pairs*

Pose these problems:

$$632 - 499 \qquad 226 - 98$$

"Is there a way we could use our conjecture/claim about subtraction to make these problems easier to solve?"

Take student ideas. Record them as equations:

$$632 - 499 = 633 - 500$$

$$226 - 98 = 228 - 100$$

Say something like, "You can use our conjecture to make some subtraction problems easier to solve. Look at the problems on this sheet. Choose at least three that you think will be easy to solve by applying our claims, and write down the equivalent problem you would use for each one. Choose at least three that you would solve another way. Be ready to say why you chose the ones you'd solve using or not using our conjecture and why."

Students work individually or in pairs on the Session 26 Student Sheet.

For the next session: Students should keep their work to bring to the next session.

1. Find at least three of these problems that you would solve using the class conjectures about subtraction. Show how you would change the problem to make it easier to solve.

2. Find at least three of these problems you would solve a different way. Be ready to explain your choices.

| | | |
|---|---|---|
| $100 - 25$ | $48 - 29$ | $86 - 23$ |
| $90 - 27$ | $91 - 29$ | $102 - 99$ |
| $102 - 68$ | $244 - 39$ | $229 - 108$ |
| $698 - 499$ | | |

See page 129.

SESSION **27** Application

*Whole class*

Discuss the problems from Session 26.

"What are examples of problems you'd solve by using our claim about addition to make an easier problem? What are examples of problems you would solve in some other way?"

This discussion can be lively. Students may disagree on which problems they would solve using the class conjectures/claims about subtraction and which problems they would solve in other ways. This makes sense because different students are comfortable with different strategies and with fluency in adding or subtracting to transform problems. Students may also point out that a combination of strategies can be useful.

As with the addition work, the points to be reinforced here are that: (1) looking at a problem as a whole before you try to solve it can help you pick a strategy appropriate for that problem; (2) transforming a problem into an equivalent, easier problem can be a very useful strategy, but you need to evaluate whether it helps in a particular case; (3) there are indications that might help you choose when to use this strategy—for example, if the amount subtracted is close to a multiple of 10 (let students suggest other tips); (4) no one strategy is best for all problems; what really helps with computation is to have several strategies you can rely on and apply as appropriate.

## SESSION 28 : Comparing Operations

### Whole class

Put up the class conjectures/claims, the ones for addition and the ones for subtraction.

Ask, "Why are there different claims for addition and subtraction? Why does it work differently when you create equivalent expressions in addition from when you create equivalent expressions in subtraction?"

After some discussion, you may want to have students write individually in response to this question as a way to end this work.

TEACHER NOTE **1** **Students' Story Contexts for Equivalent Addition Expressions**

In Session 6, students are asked to create story problems to represent 4 + 20, 5 + 19, and 6 + 18. They are asked to start with a story problem for 4 + 20 and then change the story "just enough" so that it represents 5 + 19, and then 6 + 18.

As you consider the students' stories and decide what to share in Sessions 7 and 8, keep in mind that the focus is on these three related actions: one addend increases by 1, one addend decreases by 1, and the sum stays the same. In the discussion, encourage students to think through how their stories show why the sum *has to stay the same* when the addends change in this way. Or, another way to put this question is—to keep the sum the same, if one addend increases (decreases) by 1, why is it that the other addend must decrease (increase) by the same amount? Does the story show how the changes in the addends are related to keeping the same sum? If not, how could you revise the story to show that?

Students respond in a variety of ways to this assignment. Students have a good deal of experience with story problems, but they have generally encountered the purpose of a story problem to be: figure out what the computation is, find the answer. Here, the goal is to develop a story *context* that illustrates the relationship between the changes in the addends and the value of the sum. The purpose is not to solve the problems—it has already been established that the sum of each of these expressions is 24. Rather, in these sessions, students use the story contexts to establish why these particular expressions are equivalent.

Here are several categories of student stories:

1.  Some students write a single story that shows how the addends change but the sum remains the same. These stories show some kind of movement or transformation, so that it's possible to see how, as one addend increases by 1 and the other addend decreases by 1, there is no change to the total. Representations of these stories can eventually be generalized to show that the students' conjecture is true for any (whole) numbers. (See Teacher Note #3: Representation-Based Argument for the Addition Claim.)

    > There are 20 cats on the ground and 4 cats in the tree, and 1 leaves to go on the tree. Now there are 19 cats on the ground and 5 in the tree. Then 1 more leaves to go on the tree. Now there are 18 cats on the ground and 6 in the tree.

    > 20 people in bathing suits are on the beach. 4 people are surfing. Then 1 person leaves from the beach and goes surfing. Now there are 19 people on the beach and 5 people surfing.

2.  Some students write three parallel stories, keeping all the same words and just changing the quantities to match the three expressions, but they don't indicate a movement or change from one story to the next. The two quantities

are recreated each time. Ask students whether they can revise these stories to show how the quantities change and why the sum remains the same:

> Carlos had 4 lollipops. His brother gave him 20 more. Now he has 24 lollipops.

> Carlos had 5 lollipops. His brother gave him 19 more. Now he has 24 lollipops.

> Carlos had 6 lollipops. His brother gave him 18 more. Now he has 24 lollipops.

> Bob had $4 and he wanted to buy a certain game that was $24. Then his mom gave him $20, so he had $24, enough to buy the game.

> Bob had $5 and he wanted to buy a certain game that was $24. Then his mom gave him $19, so he had $24, enough to buy the game.

> Bob had $6 and he wanted to buy a certain game that was $24. Then his mom gave him $18, so he had $24, enough to buy the game.

3. Some students write stories that include all the right quantities and are approaching an idea about changing one expression to get the next but have some confusing elements. For example in this series of stories, it's clear how the 20 cookies decrease by 1 each time, but the second quantity does not change by 1. Rather, it is recreated as a new quantity each time:

> Aliyah had 20 cookies. Rose gave Aliyah 4 more cookies. How many cookies does Aliyah have now?

> Aliyah ate 1 of the cookies so now she has only 19 cookies. Alyssa gave Aliyah 5 cookies. How many cookies does Aliyah have now?

> Aliyah ate 1 more cookie so now she has 18 cookies. Raheim gave Aliyah 6 cookies. How many cookies does Aliyah have now?

4. Some students write three separate stories. These may be related in some way, for example by topic (the first set below is all about puppies), but they don't show how a situation changes when one quantity increases and the other decreases. Or, in some stories, the two quantities are different objects (as in the second set below), so that moving an object from one group to the other or transforming both groups by the same amount does not have the potential to make the same logical sense as the stories in the other categories.

> 20 puppies were at the pet store. A girl found 4 more. How many puppies do they have now?

> 19 puppies ran away from the pet store. 5 other puppies ran away from the pet store. How many puppies ran away?

18 puppies like Doggy Dog Food. 6 puppies like Yummy Dog Food. How many puppies are there?

Kyla saw 20 cars and 4 trucks. How many did she see in all?

Kyla saw 19 cars and 5 trucks. How many did she see in all?

Kyla saw 18 cars and 6 trucks. How many did she see in all?

Eventually you will be asking students to use these contexts to think about how to prove their claim for any (whole) numbers. As you select stories, think about these questions:

- Which students' stories have the potential to be generalizable to prove their claim for any numbers?

- Which students' stories come close to being generalizable but may need some revising?

- Which students' stories give parallel problems that are correct but do not show how the changes in the addends affect the value of the sum?

Because of students' past experience with story contexts, it is not surprising that many students' stories fall into Categories 2, 3, and 4. In some classrooms, you may not have any examples like those in Category 1. If not, help students revise some of their stories to show how the changes of the two quantities are related to each other and to the sum. Here is one example:

Carlos had 4 lollipops. His brother gave him 20 more. Now he has 24 lollipops.

Carlos had 5 lollipops. His brother gave him 19 more. Now he has 24 lollipops.

Carlos had 6 lollipops. His brother gave him 18 more. Now he has 24 lollipops

Ask, "How do you know the sum has to be 24 each time without adding up the numbers? . . . Is there a way we could use the lollipop example to show why the total doesn't change? . . . Let's say I don't believe you that 5 and 19 more is 24, and I don't want to do the addition. If I know that 4 lollipops plus 20 lollipops is 24, is there a way you can show me with the lollipops that 5 plus 19 lollipops is still 24?"

The purpose of these questions is to help students consider how the first problem can be transformed into the second. Students might say, "It has to still be 24. Look, if I take 1 off the 20 and put it onto the 4, I didn't eat any lollipops. They're just in different groups," or "If Carlos has 5 lollipops, he has 1 more than he did before, so his brother has to give him 1 less."

You might say, "Could we have the lollipops on 2 plates? Let's say there are 4 on one plate and 20 on the other plate. [Draw a picture of this.] We know there are 24 lollipops. How would you change this picture so it shows 5 + 19?"

In many classes, some story contexts have emerged as particularly useful for the students to continue to consider as they work on proving their claim. Look for whether one or two of the story contexts seem to be especially powerful for many students in understanding the relationship between the changes in the addends and the value of the sum. For example, in one class, the "people in bathing suits" problem became one that the students and teacher referred to often. The people might be in the water or on the beach, but the total number didn't change. In another class, the idea of cookies on two plates was particularly useful. Cookies could be moved from one plate to the other, but the total number of cookies stayed the same.

TEACHER NOTE **2** **Representations of Equivalent Addition Expressions**

In Sessions 10–11, students create representations in order to show why it must be true that two expressions, such as 14 + 6 and 15 + 5, are equivalent.

1.  One common representation is with cubes:

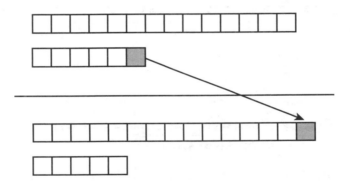

One cube is moved from the stick of 6 cubes to the stick of 14, resulting in a stick of 15 and a stick of 5.

2.  Some students might draw a picture connected to a story context:

I have two boxes of books. One has 14 books and one has 6 books. I take 1 book from the box with 6 and put it into the other box. Now one box has 15 books and the other has 5 books. But there is still the same number of books in all.

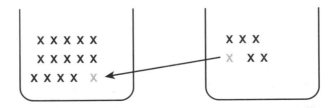

Some students might use a similar picture that is not connected to a story context, using *X*s or squares or some other simple shape.

**3.** Students might use a number line:

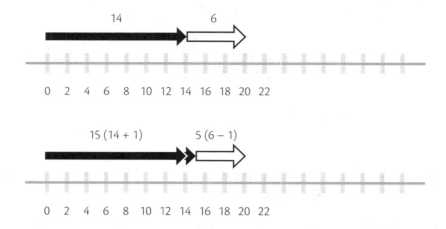

Two jumps on the number line, one of 14, starting at 0, and the next jump of 6 show a sum of the combined jumps as 20. Extending one jump by 1 to 15 and decreasing the second jump by 1 results in landing at the same place on the number line.

## TEACHER NOTE 3 Representation-Based Argument for the Addition Claim

In the Algebra and Proof sequences, students are asked to articulate conjectures about the behavior of the operations and then create representation-based arguments for their conjectures. Such arguments are based on representations accompanied by student explanations of how the representation can support the generalization. That is, students must be able to explain how their representations have the following characteristics. These will be useful to you as you analyze the student arguments:

- The meaning of the operation(s) involved in the claim is represented with diagrams, manipulatives, or story contexts.

- The representation can accommodate a class of instances (for example, all whole numbers).

- The conclusion of the claim follows from the structure of the representation; that is, the representation shows *why* the statement must be true.

Note that a static representation drawn on a page is not necessarily adequate as a representation-based argument without an accompanying explanation, which often includes a description of motions or rearrangements. This is also true of a physical model, such as one built with cubes: The student may need to show the motions of the cubes to completely explain the logic of the proof.

In Session 10, students are challenged to use their representations to prove their conjecture that if 1 is added to one addend and subtracted from the other addend, the sum remains the same. Later, in Session 14, some students work on proving the conjecture that if some amount is added to one addend and the same amount is subtracted from the other addend, the sum remains the same.

In Teacher Note 2: Representations of Equivalent Addition Expressions, the cubes, the pictures, and the number line show the meaning of addition as joining. This satisfies the first characteristic in the list above.

All of the representations also have the second characteristic. They can all accommodate the class of whole numbers. Although each representation shows particular numbers, one can imagine the number of cubes, or the number of books, or the length of the jumps on the number line as being any amounts. Students might say, "It doesn't matter how many cubes are in my two trains. I could put these behind my back and you wouldn't be able to see how many are in each, and I could still take a cube off one train and put it on the other," or, "In my story, I can have any number of books in each box. I can even start with one box that has some books and one box that has no books." Note that these representations accommodate whole numbers. If, at a later time, students wanted to expand their claim to include fractions or negative numbers, they would have to reconsider their representations. The number line would accommodate both fractions and negative numbers, but there cannot be fractions or negative amounts of cubes or books.

Finally, each of the representations can be used to show how the premise of the claim—that 1 (or some amount) is added to one addend and 1 (or the same amount) is subtracted from the other addend—leads logically to the conclusion, that the sum does not change, no matter what the addends are. For the picture of cubes, students might say, "When I move 1 cube [or some amount of cubes] from one addend to the other, it doesn't matter how many cubes I started out with in the two trains. I still have the same total number of cubes." One student pictured this idea like this:

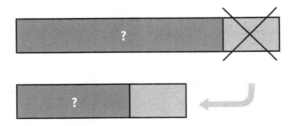

Or, for the story context, the student might say, "I can have any number of books in each box to start with. If I move some books from one box to the other, I still have the same number of books altogether, as long as I don't add any new books or take any books away."

TEACHER NOTE **4** **Students' Story Contexts for Equivalent Subtraction Expressions**

Creating story contexts for equivalent subtraction expressions is usually much more difficult for students than creating contexts for equivalent addition expressions because it is hard to think of a context in which it makes sense for the difference to remain the same. However, with some false starts, students do come up with contexts that work, often involving fantasy and humor.

Reread the Teacher Note 1: Students' Story Contexts for Equivalent Addition Expressions. Much of what is in that note applies to subtraction as well. Some students at first write parallel problems that do not show how and why the equality of the difference must be maintained, for example:

> There are 15 people. No shark comes. The next day there are 16 people. A bad shark eats 1 person. Now there are 15. Then the next day there are 17 people, and the shark comes and eats 2 people. There are 15 left. Then the next day there are 18 people, the shark eats 3. Now the shark gets caught. It is in the aquarium.

> Tyrone has 16 balloons. 4 blew away. Now he has 12.

> Tyrone has 15 balloons and 3 blew away. Now he has 12.

In these two students' work, the context is parallel in each problem, but each subtraction is separate from the others. There is not yet any reason for maintaining the difference, so there is nothing to motivate reasoning about how many must be removed and how that changes as the starting number changes.

But, as students work with these kinds of contexts, they eventually come up with reasons for maintaining the difference that later help them develop their proofs. For example, in the class where a pair of students wrote the shark problem, another pair wrote:

> The cat always wants to save 15 mice for her kittens. One day there are 15 mice in the kitchen. The cat eats 0. The next day he comes back, and there are 16 mice. She eats 1. The next day there were 17. She ate 2. The more mice there are, the more she can eat.

In another classroom, students wrote:

> There were 15 chicken wings in the refrigerator, and a dog went in and took 3 to eat. He knew his owner needed only 12 for the party. The next day there were 16 chicken wings in the refrigerator, and the dog went in and took 4 to eat, and that still left 12 chicken wings for the party.

These stories lend themselves to the development of an argument because they raise the question: As the number of original things (mice, chicken wings) changes, how must the amount eaten change in order to maintain the same difference? These kinds of contexts have helped students visualize how their claim about equivalent subtraction expressions works and why it is true.

If students are not coming up with subtraction contexts that will lend themselves to illustrating why the difference is maintained as the numbers in the problem increase or decrease by the same amount, you might want to introduce a context such as the mice. Another one that has worked well to spark students' ideas is a context about balloons.

> Katie is holding 15 helium balloons to hold her up in the air just a little off the ground. If she has too many balloons, she starts going up too high, and she has to let some go so that she always has 15. So if she has 16, she has to let the extra 1 go. If she has 17, now she has 2 extra and she has to let 2 go.

The story contexts by themselves do not yet explain why the equivalence has to hold. But by using representations based on these stories, students can develop representation-based arguments for their conjectures (see Teacher Notes 5 and 6).

## TEACHER NOTE **5** Representations of Equivalent Subtraction Expressions

In Session 21, students are asked to develop a story context and a representation for $15 - 3$ and $16 - 4$. The most common student model of subtraction is removal or, as they often say, "take away." Contexts and representations students create are often about some kind of removal.

For subtraction, like addition, representing the operation often requires more than the static representation on the page or model on the table. The representation includes both the picture or model and the student's explanation and/or demonstration of how it shows subtraction. Like the story contexts themselves, some student representations show each problem separately, side by side, without illustrating the relationship between them. Other representations (along with the student explanations) show how the starting amount and the amount subtracted changes and the effect of these changes on the difference. Between these two possibilities are a range of representations, many of which are on their way toward being representation-based arguments but are not yet quite complete.

In each of the categories below is one illustration of a "side-by-side" representation of the two expressions and one illustration of a representation that has the potential to become a representation-based argument. In Teacher Note 6: Representation-Based Argument for the Subtraction Claim, you will find examples of how the representations shown here can be used to prove the claim.

1. Some students use cubes to illustrate their story:

   In this representation, the first train shows $15 - 3 = 12$. The gray cubes are removed, and the white cubes remain. In the same way, the second train represents $16 - 4 = 12$. However, this representation shows no relationship between the two cube trains.

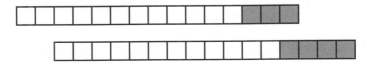

In the second cube representation, the student has lined up the two cube trains and used color to show that 1 cube is added to both the starting amount (the whole cube train) and to the part that is removed (the gray part), leaving the same difference. The student explains, "I started with 1 more, but I took 1 more away."

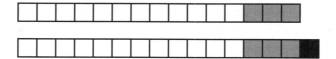

In this third representation, the student uses one cube train to represent both $15 - 3$ and $16 - 4$. The student says, "When I put 1 more on, I'm starting with 1 more, so it's 16 instead of 15, but I'm also taking away 1 more. I take away 4 instead of 3, so it's the same amount left again."

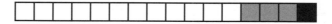

**2.** Some use pictures:

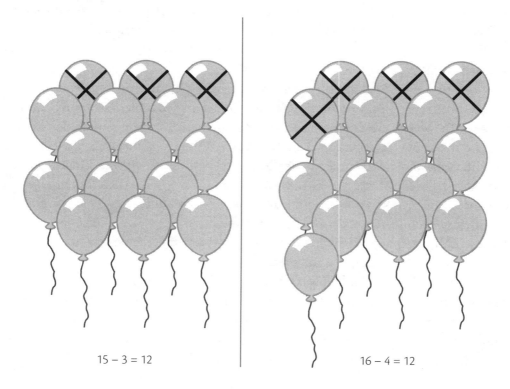

15 − 3 = 12              16 − 4 = 12

In this picture of balloons, the student represents each expression separately. In the picture of $16 - 4$, the extra balloon added at the bottom is not one of the balloons removed, so that it is difficult to see any relationship between the change in the starting amount and the change in the amount subtracted.

This student uses the position of the balloons in the picture, the color of the added balloon, and words connected to the equations to show a relationship between the two expressions:

| Has | Loses | Now Has | | Has More | Loses More | Has Same |
|-----|-------|---------|---|----------|------------|----------|
| 15 | − 3 | = 12 | | 16 | − 4 | = 12 |

**3.** Some students use number lines. (We have found fewer students who use number lines for this purpose, but there are some students who do use them successfully.) This student made several attempts at a number line, ending up with a representation like this:

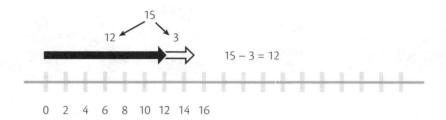

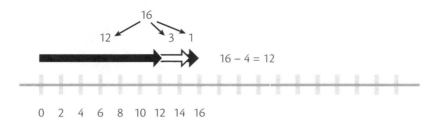

This student represents subtraction as related to addition: 15 is made up of two parts, 12 and 3. When 3 is removed, 12 remains. 16 is made up of 12 and 4 (which is shown as 3 plus an additional 1). When 4 (or 3 plus the additional 1) are removed, 12 remains.

Although we have seen few examples of students choosing to use a comparison context for their story and representation about subtraction, it is possible that some may come up in your class. For example, a possible story context and representation, using a comparison model, would be:

> Jan is 15 years old. She has a sister who is 3. Jan is 12 years older than her sister.

> A year later, Jan is 16 years old. Now her sister is 4. Jan is still 12 years older than her sister.

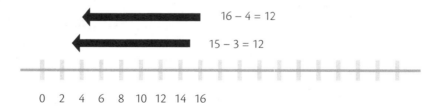

TEACHER NOTE **6** ## Representation-Based Argument for the Subtraction Claim

Reread the opening paragraphs of Teacher Note 3 about the meaning and characteristics of representation-based argument. In Sessions 23–24, students are challenged to use their representations to prove their conjecture that if 1 is added to both numbers in a subtraction expression, the difference remains the same. Some students may also be working on proving the conjecture that if the same amount is added to both numbers in a subtraction expression, the difference remains the same.

In Teacher Note 5: Representations of Equivalent Subtraction Expressions, the cubes and the pictures show the meaning of subtraction as removing an amount from a given amount. The number lines might be interpreted to show the meaning of subtraction as removal or as comparison. This satisfies the first characteristic.

All of the representations also have the second characteristic. They can all accommodate the class of whole numbers. Although each representation shows particular numbers, one can imagine the number of cubes, the number of balloons, or the length of the jumps on the number line as being any amounts. Students might say, "I could start with any number of cubes and take away any number. I could put these behind my back and you wouldn't be able to see how many cubes I start with, and I could still take some away. Then I could make it 1 cube longer to start and take away 1 more." Similarly, one can imagine starting with any number of balloons and subtracting some number of balloons, then starting with that same number plus 1 additional balloon.

Note that these representations accommodate whole numbers. If, at a later time, students wanted to expand their claim to include fractions or negative numbers, they would have to reconsider these representations. The number line can accommodate both fractions and negative numbers. For example, one can start anywhere on the number line, perhaps at $3\frac{1}{2}$, and subtract any amount, say, $\frac{3}{4}$. Or, if one starts at 3 and jumps back 5 to model $3 - 5$, the difference can be shown on the number line as $-2$. (Note: While some elementary students may be ready to understand problems involving negative numbers, complex ideas about adding and subtracting negative numbers require extended study in future grades.)

Finally, each type of representation shows the third characteristic. Each can be used to show how the premise of the claim—that 1 (or some amount) is added to (or subtracted from) both numbers in a subtraction expression—leads logically to the conclusion, that the difference does not change, no matter what the numbers are. For the second picture of cubes, students might say, "I can start out with any number of cubes and take some amount of them away. If I start all over again, but I add 1 cube [or some number of cubes] on, I can still take away the old amount plus the extras I added on, and the same amount is left as before. It doesn't matter how many cubes I started out with or the amount I take away. If I take away the old amount plus the new ones I added on, I still have the same number of cubes left." Or, for the story context, the student might say, "I can say that Katie needs any number of balloons to hold her up and she has to let the extra balloons go. So, if I give her more, she has to let that many more go."

## TEACHER NOTE 7 Algebraic Notation

Some students might be interested in using algebraic notation for articulating the conjectures in this sequence. When used correctly and with meaning, algebraic symbols are an elegant way to express mathematical relationships. However, elementary students need time and experience to make sense of this notation. Chapter 9 of *Connecting Arithmetic to Algebra* (Heinemann) is a good resource to read and reflect on both the power and the limitations of algebraic notation.

In this teacher note, we will reference ways you can incorporate algebraic notation into this sequence if you feel it is appropriate for your class or if it comes up from students. Even if algebraic notation is used, it is still important to include all of the representations, such as cube models, story situations, drawings, number lines, and statements of the claim in everyday language, so that students develop rich mental images of the operations. Whenever algebraic notation is introduced, the core questions are very important. These questions direct students to make explicit how each element of the symbolic notation is connected to the numerical instances, components of the representations, and the phrasing of the conjecture.

**Session 4**  If any students have used algebraic notation to represent their conjecture you can include that on the list, if it is correct. If students have attempted to use variables but are not able to do it correctly, don't post these attempts, but in the next session acknowledge that some students are trying to use algebraic notation and that this can be very useful. A correct way of writing the conjecture is:

$$a + b = (a + 1) + (b - 1) \text{ or, for the more general case: } a + b = (a + n) + (b - n).$$

**Session 5**  Some students might want to write the conjecture in algebraic notation, such as: $a + b = (a + 1) + (b - 1)$. If algebraic notation is included in the class conjecture, make sure there is also a version in common language.

Once students are satisfied with their statement, have them use one of the familiar examples (e.g., $6 + 9 = 5 + 10$) and the core questions, such as "What is $a$ in this example? What is $(a + 1)$? What is $b$? What is $(b - 1)$?" to make sure they know what part of the equation is meant by each part of the statement of the conjecture.

**Sessions 14–15**  As before, if some students want to write the conjecture in algebraic notation, for example, $a + b = (a + n) + (b - n)$, you can include it, but all students are not expected to make sense of this notation.

**Session 20**  If some students are interested in using symbolic notation, you can include that as one of the statements of the claim, but having a clear claim stated in words is the most important part of this session. Correct ways of using notation for the claim about adding 1 to both numbers are:

$$\text{If } a - b = c, \text{ then } (a + 1) - (b + 1) = c$$

or

$$a - b = (a + 1) - (b + 1)$$

Correct ways of using notation for the claim about adding the same amount to both numbers are:

$$\text{If } a - b = c, \text{ then } (a + n) - (b + n) = c$$

or

$$a - b = (a + n) - (b + n)$$

## SESSION 3 | STUDENT SHEET

NAME _____ DATE _____

1. Can you figure out which problems have the same sum without adding? Connect the ones with the same sum.

| | |
|---|---|
| $10 + 5$ | $11 + 13$ |
| $12 + 12$ | $49 + 26$ |
| $9 + 6$ | $17 + 19$ |
| $18 + 18$ | $50 + 25$ |

2. Write a problem that has the same sum as each of these problems. Can you do it without adding?

A.  $9 + 11$  _____

B.  $20 + 30$ _____

C.  $14 + 16$ _____

D.  $19 + 19$ _____

SESSION **17** STUDENT SHEET

NAME _____ DATE _____

1. Find at least three of these problems that you would solve using the class conjecture about adding to one addend and subtracting from the other. Show how you would change the problem to make it easier to solve.

2. Find at least three of these problems you would solve a different way. Be ready to explain your choices.

| | | |
|---|---|---|
| 25 + 75 | 99 + 9 | 49 + 51 |
| 19 + 36 | 26 + 34 | 87 + 36 |
| 45 + 63 | 90 + 70 | 229 + 56 |
| 99 + 99 + 99 | | |

**SESSION 19** **STUDENT SHEET**

NAME _____ DATE _____

1. Starting problem:      $17 - 5$

   Build off that:      _____

   Build off that:      _____

   Build off that:      _____

2. Starting problem:      $20 - 18$

   Build off that:      _____

   Build off that:      _____

   Build off that:      _____

3. Starting problem:      $25 - 5$

   Build off that:      _____

   Build off that:      _____

   Build off that:      _____

SESSION **26** STUDENT SHEET

NAME _____ DATE _____

1. Find at least three of these problems that you would solve using the class conjectures about subtraction. Show how you would change the problem to make it easier to solve.

2. Find at least three of these problems you would solve a different way. Be ready to explain your choices.

|  |  |  |
|---|---|---|
| $100 - 25$ | $48 - 29$ | $86 - 23$ |
| $90 - 27$ | $91 - 29$ | $102 - 99$ |
| $102 - 68$ | $244 - 39$ | $229 - 108$ |
| $698 - 499$ |  |  |

# B

# Changing a Number in Addition or Multiplication (Whole Numbers) [CNAM]

**Grade Range:**     Suggested for grades 3, 4, or 5

**General Claims:**   In an addition expression, if you add some amount to an addend, the sum increases by that amount.

$$a + (b + c) = (a + b) + c$$

In a multiplication expression with two factors, if you add 1 to a factor, the product increases by the other factor.

$$a \times (b + 1) = (a \times b) + a$$

In a multiplication expression with two factors, if you add some amount to a factor, the product increases by the other factor multiplied by that amount.

$$a \times (b + n) = (a \times b) + (a \times n)$$

**Number of Sessions:** Nineteen

**Teacher Notes**

1. Representation-Based Argument

2. Representations of Adding 1 to a Factor

3.  Representations of Adding Some Amount to a Factor

4.  Algebraic Notation

**Student Sheets** to accompany the following sessions: 1, 3, 6, 8, 12, 15, and 18.

## Changing a Number in Addition or Multiplication (Whole Numbers)

**General claims:**

1. In an addition expression, if you add some amount to an addend, the sum increases by that amount. For example, $2 + (3 + 5) = (2 + 3) + 5$. This is the associative property of addition. Using everyday language, some students have stated the conjecture:

   - The number that you added to an addend, take it and add it to the original sum.

   - However much is added to the addend is added to the sum.

   - When some amount is added to one of the addends, the amount you added goes onto the sum.

2. In a multiplication expression with two factors, if you add 1 to a factor, the product increases by the other factor. For example, $3 \times (4 + 1) = (3 \times 4) + 3$. Possible student language for this claim:

   - If you increase a factor by 1, you add one more of the other factor to the product.

   - If you add 1 to either the first or second factor, you increase the amount by 1 times the other factor.

3. In a multiplication expression with two factors, if you add some amount to a factor, the product increases by the other factor multiplied by that amount. For example, $4 \times (10 + 3) = (4 \times 10) + (4 \times 3)$. This is the distributive property of multiplication over addition. Students might express the claim this way:

   - If you increase one factor by any number, you have to add that amount times the other factor to the product.

## Goals for Students

The lessons in this sequence provide opportunities to work on a range of mathematical issues, depending on the needs of individual students. Although all students will be engaged in the same activities, different students will take away different learnings. For example, some students need further work in building an understanding of what multiplication is. These students will have plenty of opportunity to create representations of multiplication using relatively small numbers. Many students can model multiplication but haven't thought explicitly about how multiplication is different from addition; some of the lessons in the sequence address this issue directly. Some students will take on the challenge of choosing language to articulate conjectures with precision and then proving those conjectures.

## Sequence Overview

The first four sessions of this nineteen-session sequence provide opportunities for students to notice, articulate, represent, and make arguments about what happens when you add 1 to an addend. Sessions 5 through 10 repeat that process of noticing, articulating, representing, and making arguments as students examine what happens when you add 1 to a factor. Session 11 focuses on comparing the different claims for addition and multiplication.

In Sessions 12 through 14 students extend their investigation to consider what happens when any amount is added to a factor. Session 15 through 17 provide opportunities for students to make connections between the claim and computational strategies. In the final two sessions of the sequence, students contrast the operations of addition and multiplication based on their work with the two conjectures in the earlier lessons.

A key to helping students develop their arguments is to periodically work at making explicit the links between the numerical expressions, the story situations, the cube models, the visual drawings or number lines, and the components of the claim written in words. Embedded in the sessions are core questions, which are designed to support making these connections across the representations, the number symbols, and the claim. Even if it seems your students are making sense of the articulations of the claim and believe it to be true, asking the core questions helps students shift from a focus on what is happening with the numbers to noticing and articulating how the operation behaves.

Following the entire sequence of sessions allows students to fully investigate and make arguments for these claims using the set of whole numbers (0, 1, 2, 3, 4 . . .). After a claim is established for the set of whole numbers, depending on grade level and experience, some classes might want to continue this work beyond the nineteen sessions to see how to modify the class claims or arguments to accommodate other kinds of numbers such as fractions or integers.

## SESSION 1 : Noticing Regularity: Adding Some Amount to an Addend

*Individuals*

"We're going to start doing some sessions in mathematics that aren't part of our regular math classes. In these sessions, we will think about different things that can be said about addition and multiplication. We're going to try to figure out how to state clearly what our ideas are and how we can prove them. Because these sessions will be about generalizations and proving, we're going to call them Algebra and Proof sessions.

"Today we're going to look at some addition equations and think about what they suggest about some ways that addition works."

Present the following equations from the Student Sheet for Session 1:

| | |
|---|---|
| 12 + 8 = 20<br>14 + 8 = 22 | 12 + 8 = 20<br>12 + 10 = 22 |
| 38 + 45 = 83<br>43 + 45 = 88 | 38 + 45 = 83<br>38 + 50 = 88 |

**1.** What do you notice in the following equations?

| | |
|---|---|
| 12 + 8 = 20<br>14 + 8 = 22 | 12 + 8 = 20<br>12 + 10 = 22 |
| 38 + 45 = 83<br>43 + 45 = 88 | 38 + 45 = 83<br>38 + 50 = 88 |

**2.** When some amount is added to an addend, I think this happens to the sum: _____ .

Provide this prompt: "When some amount is added to an addend, I think this happens to the sum:_____."

See page 150.

Review with the class what is meant by the terms, *addend* and *sum*.

Tell students that they are going to each write a general statement about what is happening with these pairs of problems. Their job is to write a statement that is as clear as possible so that if people who aren't in the class read the statement, they would understand.

For the next session: Select four or five statements to post in the next session. When selecting student work to share, consider the following question: Which articulations include components that will be useful to include in a class statement of the conjecture?

It is likely that some of your students' statements will be similar, so choose some that represent a range of wording choices and ideas, including statements that capture the change in addends from one problem in the pair to the next; statements that capture the amount and or direction of the change; statements that note the systematic change in sum from one problem in the pair to the next; statements that link the change in addend to the change in sum from one problem in the pair to the next; statements that refer explicitly to the addition; statements that describe adding 1 but do not mention what happens to the sum; statements that are correct but incomplete; and so on.

Here are some examples representing this range of responses:

- You add 1 to one number and 1 to the sum.

- One number goes up and one number stays the same, the sum changes, too.

- 9 + 6. I add 1 to the 9 to make it 10 + 6, and I add 1 to the 15 to make it 16.

- If you add 1 to an addend, the sum increases by 1.

- In addition, if you change one number by 1, you change the sum by 1.

SESSION **2** : **Articulating a Conjecture**

*Whole class*

Post some of the students' statements from Session 1.

Introduce the word *conjecture*. A conjecture is a statement in mathematics that we think is true but has not been proved. "All of these statements are conjectures. We haven't yet proved that they are true for all numbers." Let the students know that you are now going to work on developing a clear class conjecture. "We need to be clear about what our conjecture is before we try to prove it."

The class looks at the statements you have listed. Read the various statements aloud. Which parts of the statements are especially useful or clear to them? One way to say this is: "Which of these statements, or parts of these statements, would help people who haven't been part of the work we've been doing so far understand our conjecture?"

As students offer their ideas, note the use of terms like *addend* and *sum*. If these terms are not used, offer them yourself. "As I was watching you write your statements in the last session, some of you were trying to remember the mathematical words that are used for addition. Here are some mathematical terms that might be useful as we try to make our conjecture clear." Put up an addition statement, such as $6 + 9 = 15$, and make sure students can identify the addends and the sum.

Work together to write a statement that will be the class conjecture.

Once students are satisfied with their statement, have them use a specific instance such as $6 + 9 = 15$ and $6 + 10 = 16$ to make sure they know what part of the equations is meant by each part of the statement of the conjecture.

Note: You may find that students continue to come up with improvements to make the conjecture clearer and more precise. You can continue revising the conjecture as the sequence continues.

Ask the class, "Is this conjecture true for all numbers, no matter which numbers we choose as addends?" Get a few students' thoughts, and let them know that this is a question the class will investigate further.

SESSION **3** : **Representing the Conjecture**

*Pairs*

Review the class conjecture. "We are pretty sure our conjecture is true, but we still need to prove that it's *always* true, no matter what numbers we choose. To do that, we're going to work with some representations to see if they will give us a way to show that it *has* to work.

"To start, we'll work with specific numbers. Then I want you to think about how you can use your representation to show it has to work for *all* numbers."

Present the following equations from the Student Sheet for Session 3:

$$9 + 5 = 14$$

$$9 + 6 = 15$$

Ask students to create a representation or story context for $9 + 5 = 14$. Then change it just enough to show $9 + 6 = 15$.

Tell students that they can use a variety of representations. They might draw a picture, draw a number line, use cubes, or create a story context.

As they work, pose questions such as these to help students focus on representations that accommodate all numbers:

> $9 + 5 = 14$
>
> $9 + 6 = 15$
>
> 1. Create a representation to show the first equation. Then change your representation just enough to show the second equation.
>
> 2. How do you need to change your representation to show that it works for other addends?
>
> 3. How does your representation prove the conjecture?

See page 151.

"How would the representation have to change to show other numbers?"

"How does the representation show the conjecture must be true for all numbers?"

Select representations to discuss in the next session. In selecting representations, consider the following criteria:

- Which selection of students' work samples shows a variety of representations? The class should be building a repertoire of representations.

- Which representations illustrate ideas to discuss? Consider in which order to present the representations to develop the ideas.

- Whose work has not been seen recently?

See Teacher Note 1: Representation-Based Argument.

# SESSION 4 : Proving the Conjecture

*Whole class*

For each representation selected from the previous session, pose the following core questions:

- How does the representation show addition?

- How does it show adding some amount to an addend?

- How does it show the impact on the sum?

- How does it illustrate our conjecture?

- Can we use the representation to explain why the conjecture must be true for all numbers?

If students have a hard time with the last question, ask if the representation can be used to explain why the conjecture must be true for other numbers. Once they have extended the idea to other addends, move back to the question of whether they can make a claim about *all* addends.

Some students might say, "It works for the cases we tried, so it must always be true." This process does not constitute proof in mathematics. Other students might say, "We don't have enough cubes to try it for all numbers, so we can't say if it will always be true." These students realize that it's not enough to say that if it works a few times, it must always be true. This stage of learning is important because students understand that when dealing with an infinite set of numbers there will always be numbers that they haven't tested yet for which the conjecture may not work. These students are articulating something important about mathematics. However, they believe the only way to determine if something is true about the operations is to perform the calculation and see if it comes out right. Therefore, they believe, one can never make a claim about an infinite set, such as all whole numbers. It is likely your class will include students with a range of beliefs about mathematical argument. These lessons are designed to support students in understanding the nature of mathematical arguments.

Still other students might say (referring to two stacks of cubes representing the two addends), "It doesn't matter how many are in each stack to start. If you add some amount to one of the stacks, you increase the sum by that amount." These students understand that they can make a claim about all numbers because this is the way addition has to work. Such a statement would constitute a convincing argument.

After the class has discussed a convincing argument, ask students which numbers work in the argument. Does it work for all whole numbers? Does it work for fractions, too? If the students are convinced they have proved their conjecture for all whole numbers but aren't sure if it works for fractions, edit the claim to say so. In this sequence, you will focus only on whole numbers (positive integers and 0). Once a class has developed an argument for all whole numbers, depending on grade level and experience with concepts of fractions, students might enjoy the challenge to investigate how to modify their representations to accommodate other numbers.

Note: Using algebraic notation is not a focus of this sequence. However, some students may bring up ideas about notation. If any students use algebraic notation to represent their conjecture, you can post that if it is correct. See Teacher Note 4: Algebraic Notation for more information and guidance.

SESSION **5** : **Noticing and Representing Regularity— Adding 1 to a Factor**

*Whole class*

"In our Algebra and Proof sessions up to now, we have been investigating what happens when you start with an addition expression and then add some amount to an addend. Now we're going to investigate what happens when we start with a multiplication expression and then add some amount to a factor. We'll be thinking about whether multiplication works like addition, or if something else happens.

"Let's first look at what happens when you add 1 to a factor. What do you notice?"

Present these two pairs of equations:

$$4 \times 6 = 24 \qquad\qquad 4 \times 6 = 24$$

$$5 \times 6 = 30 \qquad\qquad 4 \times 7 = 28$$

Have students talk to a partner to see if they notice anything in the number patterns. Elicit a few ideas. At this point, don't worry about clear articulation of a conjecture. That will come in a later session.

"In order to investigate what's going on with these patterns, we're going to think about some story contexts."

Have students talk to a partner to generate a story context for $4 \times 6 = 24$.

Elicit a few of the story contexts. Then focus on one context you have chosen because it works well mathematically. The context should be in the form of 4 groups, each group with 6 items. The context should also make sense both if you add 1 group and if you add 1 to each group. See Teacher Note 2: Representations of Adding 1 to a Factor.

Ask how the context can be used to show $4 \times 6$. Then ask the class, "How can you change the story just enough to match $5 \times 6 = 30$?"

Go back to the story for $4 \times 6 = 24$. Ask the class, "How can you change the story just enough to match $4 \times 7 = 28$?"

Make sure students notice that increasing one factor changes the number of groups, while increasing the other factor changes the number in each group.

If there is time, go through the same sequence with a different story context.

SESSION **6** : **Articulating a Conjecture— Adding 1 to a Factor**

*Whole class; individuals or pairs*

Present these equations from the Student Sheet for Session 6:

$$7 \times 3 = 21$$

$$8 \times 3 = \underline{\quad}$$

Ask the whole class, "How do you use the first equation to solve the second?"

After a few students have contributed ideas, tell students they will talk more about this in the next session. Students then work on the Student Sheet individually or in pairs.

Collect student work and select articulations to share in the next session.

$7 \times 3 = 21$

$8 \times 3 = \underline{\quad}$

$7 \times 3 = 21$

$7 \times 4 = \underline{\quad}$

1. When I add 1 to the first factor, then this happens to the product: _____.

2. When I add 1 to the second factor, then this happens to the product: _____.

See page 152.

SESSION **7** : **Articulating the Conjecture— Adding 1 to a Factor**

*Whole class*

Share some of the articulations from the previous session. Ask, "What do you see in these statements that you would want to include in our class statement?"

Work to articulate a class conjecture.

After the conjecture is articulated, ask, "For which numbers do you think our conjecture will work?"

# SESSION 8 : Representing Regularity— Adding 1 to a Factor

*Individuals or pairs*

Review the class conjecture about adding 1 to a factor. "We're going to test our conjecture with other numbers and create stories and representations to see how it works."

Students work on the Student Sheet for Session 8.

As you interact with students while they work, ask, "How does your story and diagram or array illustrate our conjecture?"

Collect their work and select some of the sets of stories and representations (a set includes the stories or representations for three equations) to present to the class.

$3 \times 5 = 15$  $3 \times 5 = 15$
$4 \times 5 = 20$  $3 \times 6 = 18$

Create a story situation for $3 \times 5 = 15$.

Draw a diagram or an array to match your story.

| Change the story just enough to show $4 \times 5$. | Change the story just enough to show $3 \times 6$. |
|---|---|
| Change your diagram or array just enough to show $4 \times 5$. | Change your diagram or array just enough to show $3 \times 6$. |

See page 153.

# SESSION 9 : Investigating with Representations— Adding 1 to a Factor

*Whole class*

Review the class conjecture. "Today we are going to look at the story contexts and diagrams you created to examine how the conjecture works."

Present the sets of stories and representations you selected. Make sure the selection includes at least one picture of groups and one array.

For each set of stories and representations, ask the core questions:

- Does this show an example of our conjecture?

- How does it show multiplication?

- How does it show changing one of the factors by 1?

- How does it show the change in the product?

SESSION **10** **Constructing an Argument: Adding 1 to a Factor**

*Whole class*

Remind students of how they were using story contexts and diagrams to show how examples of their conjecture work and why those examples work. Ask, "Would we have to test every multiplication problem to see if our conjecture works with those numbers?"

Take a few comments from the students in response to this question.

Select a story context and diagram or array from the previous session to present to the class.

Say, "This shows how our conjecture works if we start with the equation $3 \times 5 = 15$. How can we think about the story or the diagram (or array) to show that the conjecture works no matter what equation we start with?"

As the students explain how this works, emphasize the core questions:

- How do we see multiplication, no matter what the original factors?

- How do we see adding 1 to a factor, no matter what the original factors?

- Does it matter which factor you're changing?

- How do we see the change in the product, no matter what the original factors?

After the students have examined the arguments, ask them to consider whether their argument is about all whole numbers or whether they've made an argument for other kinds of numbers (like fractions) as well. Most likely, their argument is about *whole numbers* of groups and *whole numbers* of objects in each group, and the class claim should indicate that. In this sequence, the focus has been on whole numbers (positive integers and 0). Once a class has developed an argument for all whole numbers, some students, depending on grade level and experience with concepts of fractions, might enjoy the challenge to investigate how to modify their representations to accommodate other numbers.

SESSION **11** **Contrasting Operations: Adding 1 to an Addend vs. a Factor**

*Whole class*

Review the two claims, the first about addition, the second about multiplication.

Ask, "What happens when 1 is added to an addend?" "What happens when 1 is added to a factor?" "Why does something different happen when you're adding than when you're multiplying?"

This may take only a few minutes, in which case you can move on to the next session.

SESSION **12** **Expanding the Conjecture:**
**Adding Some Amount to a Factor**

*Individuals or pairs*

"We have shown what happens when 1 is added to a factor. Now we're going to investigate what happens when another number is added to a factor. How does the product change?"

Present the Student Sheet for Session 12. Collect work and select samples to share in the next two sessions. See Teacher Note 3: Representations of Adding Some Amount to a Factor.

**1.** When I add 2 to a factor, then this happens to the product: _____.

| | |
|---|---|
| $7 \times 3 = 21$ | $7 \times 3 = 21$ |
| $7 \times 5 = 35$ | $9 \times 3 = 27$ |

**2.** When I add 5 to a factor, then this happens to the product: _____.

| | |
|---|---|
| $7 \times 3 = 21$ | $7 \times 3 = 21$ |
| $7 \times 8 = 56$ | $12 \times 3 = 36$ |

See page 154.

SESSION **13** **Articulating the Expanded Conjecture**

*Whole class*

Present some of the articulations from the previous session about adding 2 or adding 5 to a factor. Have students read them aloud.

"What do you think will happen if 3 is added to a factor? What do you think will happen if 10 is added to a factor?"

Ask if students could offer a conjecture about what happens if *some amount* is added to a factor. If they have trouble getting started, present the prompt, "When I add some amount to a factor, then this happens to the product: _____."

Give students a few minutes to think about this individually or in pairs. Then elicit ideas from the class and have students create a class conjecture.

SESSION **14** **Constructing an Argument for the**
**Expanded Conjecture**

*Whole class*

Share a few sets of representations from Session 12.

For each representation set, ask the core questions:

• How do we see multiplication?

- How do we see adding 2 (or 5) to a factor?

- Does it matter which factor you're changing?

- How do we see the change in the product?

- What if we added some other amount to a factor? How do we see the change in the product? Does it match our conjecture?

- These representations start with $3 \times 7$. What if we started with some other factors? What would happen?

## SESSION 15 : Applying the Conjecture

### Individuals

Students work on the Student Sheet for Session 15.

---

**1.** $7 \times 7 = 49$. How can you use the class claim to figure out $8 \times 7$?

**2.** $8 \times 10 = 80$. How can you use the class claim to figure out $8 \times 13$?

**3.** $10 \times 18 = 180$. How can you use the class claim to figure out $14 \times 18$?

**4.** $20 \times 36 = 720$. How can you use the class claim to figure out $23 \times 36$?

---

See page 155.

## SESSIONS 16–17 : Applying the Conjecture

### Whole class

From the previous session, select a problem that almost all the students solved correctly. Ask the students to explain how they used the claim to solve the problem. Then ask them to think of a story or diagram to show how it works. Give students two minutes to think about this individually, and then elicit suggestions from the class.

Select another problem that was more challenging for the class as a whole. Ask students to explain how their claim could be applied to help them solve the problem. Have them create a story or diagram to illustrate the problem.

## SESSION 18 : Contrasting Operations

### Individuals or pairs

Post the class addition and multiplication claims.

"A few sessions ago, we discussed why something different happens when we add 1 to a number in an addition expression than when we add 1 to a number in a multiplication expression. Now our claims are more general. We've considered what happens when we add *any* amount to an addition or multiplication expression. Today you're going to draw some representations to explain why the general claims have to be different."

Students work on the Student Sheet for Session 18.

1. How does our claim for addition work for these equations?

$$4 + 3 = 7$$

$$4 + 8 = 12$$

2. Create a representation for the first equation, and then show how it changes when 5 is added to the second addend.

3. How does our claim for multiplication work for these equations?

$$4 \times 3 = 12$$

$$4 \times 8 = 32$$

4. Create a representation for the first equation, and then show how it changes when 5 is added to the second factor.

5. *Why* must the claim for addition be different from the claim for multiplication?

See page 156.

## SESSION 19 : Contrasting Operations

### Whole class

Present one of the students' representations to illustrate the claim for addition and ask the class how it shows the claim.

Present one of the students' representations to illustrate the claim for multiplication, and ask the class how it shows the claim.

Discuss as a whole group: *Why* must the claim for adding any amount to one of the numbers in an addition expression be different from adding any amount to a number in a multiplication expression?

TEACHER NOTE **1** **Representation-Based Argument**

In the Algebra and Proof sequences, students are asked to articulate conjectures about the behavior of the operations and then create representation-based arguments of their conjectures. Such proofs are based on representations accompanied by student explanations of how the representation can support the generalization, that is, students must be able to explain how their representations have the following characteristics. These will be useful to you as you analyze the student arguments:

- The meaning of the operation(s) involved in the claim is represented with diagrams, manipulatives, or story contexts.

- The representation can accommodate a class of instances (e.g., all whole numbers).

- The conclusion of the claim follows from the structure of the representation, that is, the representation shows *why* the statement must be true.

For example, consider the first conjecture in this sequence: If you add some amount to an addend, the sum increases by that amount.

Prior to creating a proof, students are asked to represent 9 + 5 and 9 + 6. A representation might look like this:

The student explains how addition is shown as the joining of two sets, addressing the first characteristic in the list above. In the first row, a set of 9 elements is joined to a set of 5 elements to give a sum of 14; in the second row, a set of 9 elements is joined to a set of 6 elements resulting in a total of 15. The representation shows what changes when 5 is changed to 6: The picture stays the same except that one black circle is added to the second set. When the circle is added to one set, it also increases the combined amount by 1.

With this image, we can see that the two sets can be any amount—the representation accommodates any positive whole number. This addresses the second characteristic. Finally, we can see from the structure of the representation that the representation has the third characteristic: When one set is increased by 1, the combined amount is necessarily increased by 1 (or, more generally, if either set is increased by some amount, the combined amount is increased by that same amount).

When selecting representations to discuss in Session 4, select at least one that has these features:

- The two addends are clearly seen.

- The amount that is added is clearly seen.

A representation with these features will support a representation-based argument.

TEACHER NOTE **2** Representations of Adding 1 to a Factor

$$4 \times 6 = 24 \qquad \bigg| \qquad 4 \times 6 = 24$$

$$5 \times 6 = 30 \qquad \bigg| \qquad 4 \times 7 = 28$$

A context about groups is useful to illustrate what happens when 1 is added to a factor. For example, a student created this story:

There are 4 mermaids coming to the zoo. Each mermaid needs 6 gallons of water. How many gallons of water does the zoo need?

To change the problem to $5 \times 6$, the student wrote:

Oh! The mermaid catcher caught 1 more mermaid for the zoo. How many gallons of water does the zoo need now?

The diagram shows one more group of 6 for the number of gallons needed for the additional mermaid. When the number of groups increases by 1, the product increases by the size of one group.

To change the problem to $4 \times 7$, the student went back to the original problem.

The mermaid catcher caught 4 mermaids for the zoo. But the mermaids are very thirsty, and they each need 7 gallons of water. How many gallons of water does the zoo need?

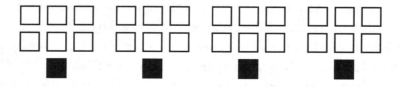

Now the diagram shows what happens when the size of a group increases by 1. The product increases by the number of groups.

In order to prove the conjecture that if you add 1 to a factor, the product increases by the other factor, students might say, "It doesn't matter how many groups I start with or how many are in each group. When I increase the first factor by 1, I add one additional group, and the product increases by the size of a group. When I increase the second factor by 1, the size of each group goes up by one, and the product increases by the number of groups."

Initially, students may find it easier to see what is happening in a picture of groups of objects. However, an array can also be used. Consider an array of 4 × 6.

For the mermaid story, each row stands for the number of gallons one mermaid drinks.

When 4 is increased by 1, one additional row is added to the array. This shows that one additional mermaid goes to the zoo—adding 6 gallons to the product.

Beginning with the 4 × 6 array, when 6 is increased to 7, one additional column is added to the array. This shows that each mermaid gets 1 extra gallon to drink – adding 4 gallons to the product.

To use these arrays for a representation-based argument, students might say, "It doesn't matter how many rows and columns I start with. If I increase the number of rows by 1, the product goes up by the number in each row. If I increase the number of columns by 1, the product increases by the number of rows."

## TEACHER NOTE 3 Representations of Adding Some Amount to a Factor

In Sessions 12–15, students consider what happens to the product when a factor is increased by a whole number amount greater than 1. They represent adding 2 or 5 to a factor. In the discussion in Session 14, students may extend their story contexts and diagrams to create representation-based arguments for the more general conjecture:

If you add some amount to a factor, the product increases by the other factor multiplied by that amount.

Consider the diagram for the mermaid story from Teacher Note 2. Starting with 4 × 6, representing 4 mermaids who each need 6 gallons of water, for each additional mermaid, the zoo will need an additional 6 gallons of water. That is, the product increases by 6 times the additional number of mermaids.

Furthermore, no matter how many mermaids you start with, and no matter how many gallons of water each mermaid needs, if the number of mermaids increases, the product (the total number of gallons needed) increases by the additional number of mermaids times the number of gallons each mermaid drinks.

Again, starting with $4 \times 6$, if the mermaids are very thirsty, the zoo will need 4 times the number of additional gallons each mermaid drinks.

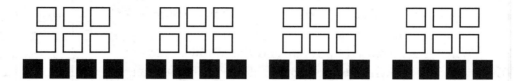

No matter how many mermaids you start with, and no matter how many gallons of water each mermaid needs initially, if each mermaid drinks more water, the product (the total number of gallons needed) increases by the number of mermaids times the additional number of gallons each of them drinks.

Picture the same situation in arrays. Start with a $4 \times 6$ array, representing the original situation of 4 mermaids, each needing 6 gallons of water.

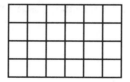

When you increase the number of rows (mermaids), the product increases by the number in each row times the number of additional rows.

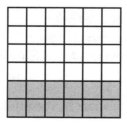

When you increase the number of columns (number of gallons), the product increases by the number of rows times the number of additional items in each row.

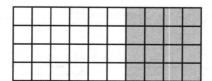

## TEACHER NOTE 4 Algebraic Notation

Some students might be interested in using algebraic notation for articulating the conjectures in this sequence. When used correctly and with meaning, algebraic symbols are an elegant way to express mathematical relationships. However, elementary students need time and experience to make sense of this notation. Chapter 9 of *Connecting Arithmetic to Algebra* (Heinemann) is a good resource to read and reflect on both the power and the limitations of algebraic notation.

In this teacher note, we will reference ways you can incorporate algebraic notation into this sequence if you feel it is appropriate for your class or if it comes up from students. Even if algebraic notation is used, it is still important to include all of the representations, such as cube models, story situations, drawings, arrays, and statements of the claim in everyday language, so that students develop rich mental images of the operations. Whenever algebraic notation is introduced, the core questions are very important. These questions direct students to make explicit how each element of the symbolic notation is connected to the numerical instances, components of the representations, and the phrasing of the conjecture.

**Session 2** One way to write this claim is "If $a + b = c$, then $a + (b + n) = c + n$." If this comes up in your class, explain that it means we can use any number in place of $a$, any number in place of $b$, and any number in place of $n$. (This can also be written as $a + (b + n) = (a + b) + n$.) At this point, the letter notation is another way to record the claim for students to see. Some students might understand it and find it useful; others may not.

**Session 7** Some students might want to write the conjecture in notation using letter symbols: $a \times (b + 1) = (a \times b) + a$. Actual algebraic notation does not use the multiplication symbol ($\times$), so writing this in correct algebraic notation is: $a(b + 1) = ab + a$. Or, if increasing the first factor by 1, the notation would be $(a + 1)b = ab + b$. A variation that students may prefer is: If $a \times b = c$, then $(a + 1) \times b = c + b$ and $a \times (b + 1) = c + a$. If algebraic notation is included in the class conjecture, make sure there is also a version in common language.

**Session 13** Some students might want to write the conjecture in notation using letter symbols: $a \times (b + n) = (a \times b) + (a \times n)$. Actual algebraic notation does not use the multiplication symbol ($\times$), so writing this in correct algebraic notation would be: $a(b + n) = ab + an$. Or, if increasing the first factor by some amount, the notation would be $(a + n)b = ab + nb$. A variation that students may prefer is: If $a \times b = c$, then $(a + n) \times b = c + n \times b$ and $a \times (b + n) = c + n \times a$. If algebraic notation is included in the class conjecture, make sure there is also a version in common language.

## SESSION **1** STUDENT SHEET

NAME _____ DATE _____

**1.** What do you notice in the following equations?

| | |
|---|---|
| $12 + 8 = 20$<br>$14 + 8 = 22$ | $12 + 8 = 20$<br>$12 + 10 = 22$ |
| $38 + 45 = 83$<br>$43 + 45 = 88$ | $38 + 45 = 83$<br>$38 + 50 = 88$ |

**2.** When some amount is added to an addend, I think this happens to the sum: _____ .

**NAME** _____ **DATE** _____

$$9 + 5 = 14$$

$$9 + 6 = 15$$

1. Create a representation to show the first equation. Then change your representation just enough to show the second equation.

2. How do you need to change your representation to show that it works for other addends?

3. How does your representation prove the conjecture?

NAME _____ DATE _____

$$7 \times 3 = 21$$

$$8 \times 3 = \underline{\phantom{00}}$$

$$7 \times 3 = 21$$

$$7 \times 4 = \underline{\phantom{00}}$$

1. When I add 1 to the first factor, then this happens to the product: _____.

2. When I add 1 to the second factor, then this happens to the product: _____.

## SESSION 8 : STUDENT SHEET

NAME _____ DATE _____

$$3 \times 5 = 15 \qquad 3 \times 5 = 15$$

$$4 \times 5 = 20 \qquad 3 \times 6 = 18$$

Create a story situation for $3 \times 5 = 15$.

Draw a diagram or an array to match your story.

| Change the story just enough to show $4 \times 5$. | Change the story just enough to show $3 \times 6$. |
|---|---|
| Change your diagram or array just enough to show $4 \times 5$. | Change your diagram or array just enough to show $3 \times 6$. |

SESSION **12** STUDENT SHEET

NAME _____ DATE _____

1. When I add 2 to a factor, then this happens to the product: _____.

$$7 \times 3 = 21 \qquad 7 \times 3 = 21$$

$$7 \times 5 = 35 \qquad 9 \times 3 = 27$$

2. When I add 5 to a factor, then this happens to the product: _____.

$$7 \times 3 = 21 \qquad 7 \times 3 = 21$$

$$7 \times 8 = 56 \qquad 12 \times 3 = 36$$

3. Create a story situation and a diagram or an array to show $7 \times 3 = 21$. Then change them just enough to show one of the other equations.

# SESSION 15 : STUDENT SHEET

NAME _____ DATE _____

1. $7 \times 7 = 49$. How can you use the class claim to figure out $8 \times 7$?

2. $8 \times 10 = 80$. How can you use the class claim to figure out $8 \times 13$?

3. $10 \times 18 = 180$. How can you use the class claim to figure out $14 \times 18$?

4. $20 \times 36 = 720$. How can you use the class claim to figure out $23 \times 36$?

## SESSION 18 : STUDENT SHEET

NAME _____ DATE _____

1. How does our claim for addition work for these equations?

$$4 + 3 = 7$$

$$4 + 8 = 12$$

2. Create a representation for the first equation, and then show how it changes when 5 is added to the second addend.

3. How does our claim for multiplication work for these equations?

$$4 \times 3 = 12$$

$$4 \times 8 = 32$$

4. Create a representation for the first equation, and then show how it changes when 5 is added to the second factor.

5. *Why* must the claim for addition be different from the claim for multiplication?

# REFERENCES

Carpenter, Thomas P., Linda Levi, Megan Loef Franke, and Julie Koehler Zeringue. 2005. "Algebra in Elementary School: Developing Relational Thinking." *ZDM* 37(1): 53–59.

Flynn, Michael. 2016. *Beyond Answers: Exploring Mathematical Practices with Young Children*. Portland, ME: Stenhouse.

National Council of Teachers of Mathematics. 2014. *Principles to Actions: Ensuring Mathematical Success for All*. Reston, VA: NCTM.

National Governors Association Center for Best Practices and Council of Chief State School Officers. 2010. *Common Core State Standards: Mathematics*. Washington, DC: National Governors Association Center for Best Practices and Council of Chief State School Officers.

National Research Council. 2001. *Adding It Up: Helping Children Learn Mathematics*. J. Kilpatrick, J. Swafford, and B. Findell (Eds.). Mathematics Learning Study Committee, Center for Education, Division of Behavioral and Social Sciences and Education. Washington, DC: National Academy Press.

Russell, Susan Jo, Deborah Schifter, and Virginia Bastable. 2011. *Connecting Arithmetic to Algebra: Strategies for Building Algebraic Thinking in the Elementary Grades*. Portsmouth, NH: Heinemann.

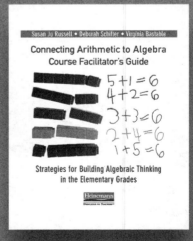